Easy Family History

The stress-free guide to starting
your research

David Annal

the national archives

First published in 2005 by
The National Archives
Kew, Richmond
Surrey, TW9 4DU, UK

www.nationalarchives.gov.uk

The National Archives (TNA) was formed when the Public Record Office (PRO) and Historical Manuscripts Commission (HMC) combined in April 2003.

ISBN 1 903365 79 1

Designed and typeset by Geoff Green Book Design
Cover designed by Penny Jones and Michael Morris
Printed by MPG Books, Bodmin, Cornwall

Contents

Picture acknowledgements

p.   8 David Annal
pp. 24, 48, 86, 194 General Register Office (Office
      of National Statistics)
p. 100 Principal Registry of the Family Division
p. 122 Shropshire Archives
p. 168 © and database right Crown Copyright and
      Landmark Information Group Ltd (All rights
      reserved 2005)
p. 180 Internet Library of Early Journals
p. 224 www.freebmd.org.uk

Introduction: Who are we? Who were they?

This book comes with an important health warning: before you start to take an active interest in your family history you should be aware that there may be no going back!

You'll soon find out that researching your family history can be highly addictive. Over the past few years this once-peaceful little hobby of ours has started to become a bit of a national obsession: articles have appeared in the national press; online releases of historical documents have brought down websites; pressure groups have been formed; and questions have even been asked in the House of Commons.

There are a number of theories as to why this outwardly bookish and academic pursuit should have caught the nation's imagination in such an extraordinary way, but the truth of the matter is that no one really knows the answer. Some look for sociological or political reasons – a growing detachment from our ancestral roots leading to a need to rediscover an idyllic past. Some put it down more simply to a natural human inquisitiveness, while others point to the growth in leisure time and the opportunities brought about by the advent of the internet and the World Wide Web. I'm sure that there's some truth in all of these theories and also that the answer is a combination of certain aspects of each.

The role of television in all this shouldn't be underestimated: in 1979, the BBC broadcast a landmark programme called, quite simply, *Family History*. Although it was essentially a personal journey (undertaken by the broadcaster Gordon Honeycombe), it struck a chord with millions of viewers and inspired a generation of family historians. The programme was groundbreaking in the way that it showed how 'ordinary' people could research documents recording the lives of their 'ordinary' ancestors to tell the story of their family. For the first time, family history was presented as a hobby that everyone could get involved in rather than being the exclusive preserve of the aristocracy.

Moving rapidly forward some twenty-five years we come to another groundbreaking television series. In October 2004, the BBC began a series of programmes following the personal journeys of ten celebrities as they set about discovering the truth about their ancestors. The public reaction to *Who Do You Think You Are?* took even the BBC by surprise as viewing figures topped five million for some of the shows – surpassing all other programmes broadcast on BBC2 that year.

Despite the great distance in time between the two series, they had several features in common. Neither Gordon Honeycombe nor any of the celebrities featured in *Who Do You Think You Are?* had any noble or titled ancestry; most came from 'normal' middle-class or working-class backgrounds. As well as telling some fascinating and moving stories, often tinged with a degree of sadness, both programmes took time to illustrate the actual process of family history research and to demonstrate how easy it was for people to set out on their own voyages of discovery.

And that's what this book aims to do. Each chapter covers a different source, looking at the background to the records, what information they contain and how to get the most out of them. On the way, we'll look at some of the problems you might encounter and suggest ways that you can work around them.

This book starts by looking at what most researchers would agree are the most important basic sources for family historians – birth, marriage and death certificates, census returns, wills and parish registers – and then goes on to look at some other resources that are fairly easily accessible

Did you know?
The Family Records Centre (FRC) opened in 1997, bringing together, under the same roof, the two most important sources for family historians in England and Wales: the General Register Office's birth, marriage and death indexes and the 19th-century census returns. The centre now receives over a thousand visitors a day.

and can provide you with additional vital information about your ancestors and the way they lived their lives.

There's an attempt to concentrate on sources that can be accessed from all parts of the country – not just London and the south east – although it's an unavoidable fact that many of the most important documents are held by the National Archives and can only be seen at Kew or at the Family Records Centre in London. But the family history centres run by the Church of Jesus Christ of Latter-day Saints, the national network of county record offices and local studies libraries and, above all else, the internet, have all helped to bring many of the most basic sources within easy reach of the vast majority of the population.

The book is unashamedly biased towards 19th-century sources since this is the period where you are likely to experience the greatest success in your research. The main focus is on the records of English and Welsh ancestors, but the majority of research techniques we'll examine are equally valid for other parts of the united Kingdom.

One very important skill that all newcomers to the mysterious world of family history should try to develop is the ability to read documents with a critical eye. You need to be able to look at them and understand not just what they say, but also what this information means to your research. Although you may well consider the discovery of your great great grandmother's birth certificate to be a fantastic achievement and a significant milestone, what is significant is not the certificate itself or the information it contains – rather, the clues that you now have to lead you on to other sources in your constant quest to uncover more and more ancestors.

But this book will also attempt to encourage you to look beyond the potentially dreary process of simply collecting names and dates for your family tree and to try to find out what life was really like for your ancestors. We'll look at a number of less well-known sources that will help you to do this.

Problem-solving is another important skill for family historians to develop. The ability to look at a problem in an objective way and to reach logical conclusions based on the evidence available to you comes in very handy. And when you feel that you've hit a brick wall, why not take a step back and see if you can work your way around it instead of trying to knock it down?

Family history is changing: the online revolution has probably affected our hobby more than any other leisure pursuit, and to reflect this a whole chapter has been dedicated to the internet. Although it is still possible to research your family history without ever setting foot in cyberspace, the number of people who are resistant to this new technology is diminishing daily. In fact, family historians are at the forefront of the Silver Surfers movement, and you might be surprised to learn how many people aged over eighty have not only come to terms with computers but are now actively spreading the word among their contemporaries.

This book attempts to get you started. It cannot, of course, cover everything: once you start to think about it, almost any document that includes a person's name could constitute a family history source; but you do have to draw the line somewhere!

One final point: throughout this book the term 'family history' has been used in preference to 'genealogy'. This is entirely a personal preference, but it's important to me. Family history is 'exactly what it says on the tin' – the history of people's families. Genealogy sounds too much like a science, too much like homework. Family history is an enjoyable, challenging, sometimes frustrating, but ultimately rewarding hobby. Yes, you should take your research seriously, you should organize your notes efficiently and keep your files and family trees up to date, but at the same time you should keep it all in perspective. It is just a hobby – you don't have to do it and you can stop whenever you want to! But for many thousands of people, researching their family history has become a lifetime's work; and once you take that first step on your voyage of discovery, there may be no looking back.

The Davidson family, ancestors of the author, photographed about 1905 in Edinburgh.

Chapter 1

Homework: your own resources

- Family history begins at home
- History in the attic
- Family treasures
- Enter, the relatives
- Checklist: interviews
- Table: Key dates for family historians

Family history begins at home

It's amazing how much you can find out about your ancestors before you even set foot in a library or a record office. You probably have lots of sources in your own home that you've never thought of as historical documents, and you almost certainly have a lot of basic information about your ancestors tucked away in that remarkable archive know as the human brain. And don't forget about your Auntie Margaret – she knows a lot more about your ancestors than you'd think, and she's probably been trying to talk to you about them for the past twenty years, but you haven't been listening, have you? Well, now's the time to start.

There's another source, available in most homes, which is rapidly changing the way we research our family history – the internet. We'll have a look at this extraordinary resource in more detail later on in the book.

So, the best place to start your research is in your own home. This is where it pays to have relatives who possessed the 'hoarding' gene. The ancestor who decided to deal with their deceased father's belongings by reducing them to cinders on a bonfire is the curse of the modern family historian. And most families will know about the old family photo album which Granny used to have, but no one's quite sure where it is now.

History in the attic

But there's a good chance you'll find that, some-where, someone in the family has got a little box in an attic with a collection of family papers. It probably won't be a large tea chest stuffed full of old legal documents recording the purchase of the house (that you still live in) by your great great grandfather 150 years ago. Very few of us will find a diary kept by our suffragette great grandmother, and you probably won't come across a bundle of letters written by your great uncle to his mother from his rat-infested World War I trench. But what you do find will prove invaluable as you set out on the trail of your ancestors.

The items you're most likely to find are copies of birth, marriage and death certificates, news-paper cuttings and perhaps an old will. You might find an ancestor's employment records, trade union or club membership cards, school reports and, if you're very lucky, that holy grail of family historians, the Family Bible.

Some of these documents will be over a

Did you know?
Most counties have at least one family history society —
it's well worth joining your local society as well as the
ones that cover the areas that your ancestors came
from. You'll get copies of journals and you can go to regular meetings where you can hear talks by experts and
share your experiences with other researchers.

hundred years old and they may be in pretty poor
condition. You would be well advised to get them
photocopied or digitally scanned as soon as possible. Don't carry the originals around with you
when you go to see relatives or visit a record
office — if you do, you'll find that old paper can
disintegrate rapidly and you run the risk of losing
valuable information. These are precious documents and they are irreplaceable. And what
makes them particularly important for family historians is that you know right from the start that
they relate to your ancestors. As you progress
with your research you'll find that proving
whether a particular birth certificate relates to
your ancestor or not is one of the most difficult
tasks facing you. These documents from your
attic have what we might call built-in provenance.
We know where they came from and we can be
pretty sure that they belonged to your direct
ancestors.

It's worth spending some time looking at these documents, reading them thoroughly for clues. Make notes about what they tell you about your family. Once you've added the parts of the family that you have in your personal knowledge, you should have enough information to draw up your first family tree. There's no right or wrong way to do this – the important thing is to record the details in a way that makes it easy for you to tell at a glance what you know about the various members of your family. And you'll probably be surprised to see how much you already know. Most people have some personal knowledge of their grandparents, aunts, uncles and cousins, and if you've been lucky with your box in the attic you might have a tree going back three or four generations – maybe even more.

It doesn't matter if you don't have a lot of family information at home – just knowing when and where you were born is enough to get you started – but you'll certainly be off to a flying start if you happen to have a good collection of family documents

Family treasures

Our Victorian and Edwardian ancestors were very keen to leave their mark on history and you may be fortunate enough to have inherited the old Family Bible, where you will find the names and dates of birth (or christening) of several generations of your family recorded. A brief note of caution here: entries in Family Bibles were often made many years after the event and therefore the dates of birth, like so many other 'facts' you'll come across while researching your family history, will need to be checked against official sources. Nevertheless, old Family Bibles really are a treasure chest, and if you don't have one yourself it's quite possible that a distant cousin may be the lucky owner.

Photographs are another great source for family historians, but frustratingly they are rarely labelled so we may end up with a wonderful collection of pictures of our Edwardian and late-Victorian ancestors with no way of knowing whether the old gentleman with the handlebar moustache is Great Uncle Bill or his cousin Harry. However, older members of the family may be able to help you put names to some of the faces, and details such as the photographer's name and address may just give you a useful clue as to which branch of the family the stern old lady in the sombre black dress came from.

Enter, the relatives

And now's the time to start getting in touch with your cousins, uncles and aunts – anyone who's related to you who might know something about the family. The ideal candidate is the great aunt in Tunbridge Wells who still lives in the house where your grandfather was born and knows all the old family stories. But beware: the relatives you get in touch with might not have any interest in family history whatsoever and they may not be too keen on talking about the past. They may even know something about the family that they don't want to share with you – an illegitimate birth or a criminal ancestor, or perhaps some event which reminds them of a time of sadness, like the death of a young child. So it's important to approach relatives in the right way and to treat them with respect and kindness. Also, it's a good idea to share your findings with your relatives right from the start. An old newspaper cutting could be the trigger that releases a whole flood of memories or a photo they haven't seen for years might remind them of an uncle who emigrated to Australia half a century ago, while a copy of their grandfather's birth certificate might reveal something they didn't know before.

Don't expect your elderly relatives to know

Checklist: interviews

Ten tips for interviewing elderly relatives.

- *Get in touch before you visit – don't turn up announced.*
- *Explain what you're doing and why you're doing it.*
- *Take copies of relevant documents and photos with you.*
- *Take notes of what your relatives say.*
- *Share your findings.*
- *Don't bombard them with too many questions.*
- *Don't behave like an interrogator.*
- *Be sensitive – there may be things they don't want to talk about.*
- *Don't expect precise information.*
- *Don't believe everything they say.*

everything about the family — most of all, don't expect them to know the precise dates of family events which took place half a century ago. A question like 'When did Uncle Stan die?' is unlikely to produce results, but if you were to ask whether Stan died before or after his brother Alf, you may just get a meaningful answer. People often associate family events with national ones, so they may remember that their great grand-father died a few weeks after Queen Alexandra, but without knowing when that was.

One of the most important things to bear in mind when dealing with family stories is that they tend to get twisted even over a fairly short period of time. We've probably all been at family gatherings where memories are being shared by distant cousins and you can almost guarantee that there will be a dispute about some detail — such as which great uncle it was who died in the battle of the Somme or whether Cousin Alice moved to Perth or Melbourne.

It's obvious how these stories can become corrupted over hundreds of years, and while there may be a grain of truth at the root of the story (and there nearly always is), it's your job as a researcher to question it and to maintain a healthy degree of cynicism. For example, was your great great grandfather really a solicitor or was he in fact a solicitor's clerk? Did your ancestor really fight at the battle of Trafalgar or did he join the crew of the *Victory* five years later? And did that great uncle actually die at the battle of the Somme? Could the story that's been passed down to you be an example of an understandable exaggeration on the part of his descendants? After all, don't we all want to think the best of our ancestors, and isn't it nice to believe that they took part in some of the greatest events in history?

Once you've gathered together all the information you can find at home and you've made contact with some aunts, uncles and cousins, it's time to start looking further afield. Later in this book we will look in some detail at the vast range of family history resources available on the World Wide Web. At this stage, it's worth having a look at some of the most important websites and familiarizing yourself with the different ways in which you might use the internet to help you piece together your family history.

Although family history has been one of the most popular internet pursuits ever since the World Wide Web started to develop, it's only in the last few years that the full potential of this vast resource has begun to be realized. The earliest family history websites were either personal sites on which enthusiastic amateur genealogists posted the results of their research, together with family photos and stories, or they were bigger, often 'official' sites, which contained indexes to records such as census returns, wills, or births, marriages and deaths. While many of these were extremely valuable and opened up whole new avenues of research, they were still no substitute for getting access to the primary source material – to the original documents that they referred to.

Today, however, all of this has changed. The internet now provides access to some of the most important family history source material, the most significant being the 19th-century census returns for England and Wales and over a million wills dating back to the 14th century. And if you're lucky enough to have Scottish forebears you are now able to view digital copies of your ancestors' birth, marriage and death certificates online from the comfort of your own home.

The internet is also home to a vast number of dedicated mailing lists and message boards, and this has allowed family history to become a truly worldwide pursuit. It's now relatively easy to get in touch with distant cousins not just in the USA, Australia, Canada and New Zealand but also in other countries where British emigrants ended up, like Argentina, South Africa or Israel. Posting

Key dates for family historians
(for England and Wales)

1538	Introduction of parish registers
1598	Bishops' transcripts – copies of parish registers sent to the bishops
1649–60	The Commonwealth period – gaps in parish registers
1732	All parish registers written in English rather than Latin
1752	Gregorian Calendar adopted
1754	Hardwicke's Marriage Act implemented, standardizing recording of marriages
1801	First national census taken
1813	Rose's Parochial Register Act implemented, standardizing recording of baptisms and burials
1837	Start of civil registration of births, marriages and deaths
1841	Earliest surviving national census returns
1858	Establishment of civil probate system
1875	Registration Act passed, tightening up certain aspects of the civil registration system
1882	Married Women's Property Act implemented – married women could now legally own property
1901	Latest available census returns

a message asking for information or offering to share information about your ancestors can produce amazing results – you never know who might read it. Simply typing a name into a good internet search engine can throw up some interesting leads, and if you're feeling really adventurous you might even think about starting your own family website.

The last thing to mention here about the internet is that most of the archives and record offices you will visit have highly informative websites that will tell you everything you need to know about planning a visit. Many of them also have online catalogues so you can check that what you want to look at is available and possibly even order it in advance.

A list of useful websites can be found at the end of this book.

Easy does it

It's understandable that when you set out on your research you will want to make as much progress as possible as quickly as you can. But there's a danger that by going too quickly you may miss important clues, and you could even end up researching the wrong family, so it's very important that you prove each link as you go. You need to be certain that the birth certificate you have found is in fact your great grand-father's and not that of someone else of the same name who happened to be born around the same time in the same place. This is not always as easy as it sounds, but it really is worth spending some of your valuable time in making sure that you're literally on the right lines.

Although there is no right or wrong way to go about your research, it's a good idea to follow a few basic principles. And the most important of these is that you should always start with the earliest well-documented event in your family and work backwards from there. For example, if you have a copy of your grandfather's birth certificate, the next step would be to trace his parents' marriage certificate. Once you have this, you can look for *their* birth certificates, and so on. Along the way you will use a variety of other sources to help you identify the correct certificates, but if you follow this basic process to move from one generation to an earlier one, you won't go far wrong.

There's also a temptation to make what we might call great 'leaps of faith', assuming that since your surname is SHAKESPEARE, or NELSON, or NIGHTINGALE you are therefore related to or even descended from the famous person of that name. Or you might have found a reference on a website to a farmer living in the 17th century who happens to have your surname and comes from the same area as you. Don't be tempted to claim him as your own before you've researched the family line thoroughly. In family history, there is no substitute for serious methodical research. Of course your research should be fun; of course you should enjoy it; but, unless you continually ask yourself whether you are certain that you can prove each step of your research, you run the very real risk of researching someone else's family history.

CERTIFIED COPY OF AN ENTRY OF BIRTH

GIVEN AT THE GENERAL REGISTER OFFICE

Application Number: PRO2001

REGISTRATION DISTRICT Bromley

1845. BIRTH in the Sub-district of Bromley in the County of Kent

Columns:	1	2	3	4	5	6	7	8	9	10
No.	When and where born	Name, if any	Sex	Name and surname of father	Name, surname and maiden surname of mother	Occupation of father	Signature, description and residence of informant	When registered	Signature of superior	Name entered after registration
	Fourth of July 1845 Bromley	George Howard	Boy	Charles Robert Darwin	Emma Darwin formerly Wedgwood	Charles Robert Darwin Gentleman	Charles Robert Darwin Father Down	Ninth of August 1845	Chas Wright	

CERTIFIED to be a true copy of an entry in the certified copy of a Register of Births in the District above mentioned.

Given at the GENERAL REGISTER OFFICE, under the Seal of the said Office, the 5th day of February 2001

BXBZ 113009

CAUTION: THERE ARE OFFENCES RELATING TO FALSIFYING OR ALTERING A CERTIFICATE AND USING OR POSSESSING A FALSE CERTIFICATE ©CROWN COPYRIGHT

WARNING: A CERTIFICATE IS NOT EVIDENCE OF IDENTITY.

BXBZ Issue: 06/2001 2346 460 ENGLAND/ED

PA

A certified copy of the 1845 birth certificate of George Howard Darwin, son of the biologist and theorist Charles Darwin and his wife Emma.

Chapter 2

In the beginning: birth records

- Civil registration – 1837 and all that
- The General Register Office indexes
- Birth certificates
  When and where born
  Name, if any
  Sex
  Name and surname of father
  Name, surname and maiden surname of mother
  Occupation of father
  Signature, description and residence of informant
  When registered and signature of registrar
  Name entered after registration
- Changes in 1969
- Searching for a birth certificate
- Non-registration of births
- Linking GRO certificates to census returns
- Checklist: birth certificate searches
- Adoptions

Civil registration – 1837 and all that

The first documentary sources that most of us come across when we start researching our family history are our ancestors' birth, marriage and death certificates. In England and Wales, births, marriages and deaths have been registered by the state since 1 July 1837. The year 1837 is therefore one of the most important dates for family historians to remember.

This process of state registration of births, marriages and deaths is known as civil registration and, along with the census returns, the records of these events form the backbone of the research into our family history. The certificates provide the basic facts about the most important events in a person's life and, crucially, give us invaluable information about our ancestors' parents, spouses and children.

Civil registration didn't begin in Scotland until 1855 and it wasn't until 1864 that comprehensive registration of births, marriages and deaths was introduced in Ireland.

In England and Wales, the country was divided up into a number of registration districts, each of which was itself divided into sub-districts. This basic structure of districts and sub-districts is still in place today, although the boundaries and the names of the districts have in many cases changed considerably.

The local registrars were responsible for registering the births and deaths that occurred in their own districts, with separate arrangements made for marriages. The relevant information about each event was entered into a register under a number of headed columns. At the end of every three months, the registrars sent details of all the births, marriages and deaths registered in their districts to the General Register Office (GRO).

Copies of birth, marriage and death certificates can be ordered in a number of different ways:

- in person from the Family Records Centre in London;
- by post or by phone from the General Register Office in Southport;
- online via the GRO's website at: *www.gro.gov.uk/gro/content/certificates*;
- by post or in person from the various local register offices – *but only for events registered in that district* – and note that the GRO's index reference numbers (i.e. the volume and page number) are of no relevance to the local registrars.

Information about current fees can be obtained from the General Register Office.

The General Register Office indexes

Once the details have been received from all the registrars in England and Wales, it's then the job of the General Register Office to compile national indexes – a job which has been carried out conscientiously and (largely) efficiently since the start of civil registration in July 1837.

A complete set of these indexes (often misleadingly referred to as the 'St Catherine's House' indexes after their former location) is now housed at the Family Records Centre in London. Copies of the GRO indexes are available on microfiche at a variety of locations including the Society of Genealogists' Library in London, Latter-day Saints' family history centres, county record offices and larger public libraries. A full list of the holders of GRO index microfiche is available on the GRO's website at: *www.gro.gov.uk/gro/content/certificates/ficheholders.asp*.

Indexes to births, marriages and deaths can also be accessed via the internet. The most useful websites are:

- *www.freebmd.org.uk* – a free site, run by volunteers who are extracting the information from the GRO indexes and creating a searchable (but not yet complete) database;
- *www.familyrelatives.org* – a pay-per-view site including a fully searchable database of births, marriages and deaths from 1866 to 1920;
- *www.1837online.com* – a pay-per-view site giving access to digital images of the pages from the GRO indexes;
- *www.bmdindex.co.uk* – a subscription site providing access to English and Welsh birth, marriage and death indexes from 1837 to 2003;
- *www.ukbmd.org.uk* – a portal site, with links to hundreds of other sites including Local BMD, which gives access to local records of births, marriages and deaths from certain parts of the country.

The FreeBMD website (see p. 224) has revolutionized the way we search for records of our ancestors' births, marriages and deaths. It's fair to say that, nowadays, anyone searching for an event registered between 1837 and 1911 should begin their search on this website. There's little to be said in favour of spending hours trawling through scores of heavy index books when you can find the information you want in a few minutes on the internet.

FreeBMD still has some way to go before it can really be said to have replaced the GRO indexes as the primary means of access to these records, but you only need to look at the sheer volume of entries (just over 100 million at the time of writing) and the sophisticated ways in which the search engine enables you to interrogate the data to see why so many family historians are logging on to this remarkable website. The days of those soul-destroying 50-year searches through the indexes are numbered.

It really doesn't matter whether you're searching online, on microfiche or in the original index books at the Family Records Centre – the same principles should always apply. And although your searches in the indexes will normally be quite straightforward, there will be occasions when the record you're looking for proves difficult to track down. The tips in the main sections on birth, marriage and death certificates in this book are designed to help you to work your way through the minefield of civil registration.

Until 1983, the GRO indexes were divided into quarterly volumes. So, for each year, there are four volumes listing the births, marriages or deaths registered in:

- January, February and March
- April, May and June
- July, August and September
- October, November and December

The quarters are commonly referred to by the name of the last month of the quarter, i.e. March (MAR), June (JUN), September (SEP) and December (DEC). Since 1984 there has been a single volume of indexes for each year.

It's important to bear in mind that the indexes are arranged by the date of *registration* rather than the date of the event itself. This isn't a major issue with marriages, which are registered on the day of the ceremony, or with deaths, which have to be registered within five days (until 1875, within eight days). However, births can be registered up to six weeks after the event, so it is not at all uncommon to find a birth listed in the 'following' quarter. For example, a child who was born towards the end of May 1867 may not have been registered until the beginning of July. In that case, the birth would be found in the index for the September quarter of 1867.

Each quarterly volume lists the names of everyone whose birth, marriage or death was registered in that quarter. The names are listed in alphabetical order, first by surname and then, within each surname, by forename. The place shown in the indexes is the name of the district in which the event was registered, which is not necessarily the actual place in which it occurred. Registration districts can cover quite a large area which may contain several different towns. For example, the registration district of Prescot in Lancashire included the towns of Eccleston, Hale, Knowsley, Prescot, St Helens, Widnes and Windle, as well as several smaller places. A birth, marriage or death occurring in any of these places would appear in the indexes as 'Prescot'.

The reference number shown in the indexes consists of a volume and a page number, and allows the GRO to identify a particular entry. The volume number identifies a wide geographical area, and although the numbers have changed over the years they remained the same from 1852 to 1946, the period of most interest to family historians. This can be a great help to those of us without an encyclopedic knowledge of English geography – all events registered in Cheshire, for example, will have a volume number of 8a.

Birth certificates

The GRO indexes give only limited information about each registered birth:

- name
- mother's maiden surname (from SEP 1911)
- registration district
- reference number (volume and page)

The basic layout of English and Welsh birth certificates and the information they contained remained the same from the first day of registration in July 1837 right up until the end of March 1969. Each certificate shows the following information:

- when and where born
- name, if any
- sex
- name and surname of father
- name, surname and maiden surname of mother
- occupation of father
- signature, description and residence of informant
- when registered and signature of registrar
- name entered after registration

In addition, at the top of the certificate, the year of registration and the names of the registration district, the sub-district and the county are recorded.

Let's have a look in more detail at each of these columns.

• *When and where born*

This column records the date and place of the child's birth. The day and month are usually written in full, followed by the year. In the case of multiple births (twins, triplets, etc.) the time of birth is also given – it is important for legal purposes (for example, inheritance of property) to know which one of a pair of twins was the older. So if you come across an English or Welsh birth certificate with a *time* of birth it's worth checking to see if there was another child registered at the same time. However, a number of registrars, particularly in the early years of civil registration, recorded the times of births as a matter of course.

The place of birth is usually quite precise, although it may just show the name of the village or small town – particularly in the early years of registration. For children born in the larger towns and cities you should expect to find the full address: house number, street and town.

- *Name, if any*

This column contains the child's forename together with any middle names. Note that the surname is not entered here: it is assumed that the child has the same surname as its father, or, if no father is shown, the same as its mother.

Occasionally this column was left blank, indicating that the parents hadn't chosen a name for the child by the time its birth was registered. The birth would be entered in the index as 'Male' or 'Female'. Sometimes a name was added later and this would be recorded in the column headed 'Name entered after registration', but often the reason for the absence of a name is that the child had died before being baptized. In such cases you would expect to find a corresponding 'Male' or 'Female' death registration.

- *Sex*

The single word 'Boy' or 'Girl' should be entered in this column, indicating the sex of the child. From 1 April 1969, the terms 'Male' and Female' are used instead.

- *Name and surname of father*

The first name, any middle names and the surname of the father will be found here. A blank space indicates an illegitimate birth. A potential problem to watch out for is that, before 1875, the mother of an illegitimate child could have the father's name recorded on the birth certificate whether or not he was there to confirm that he was indeed the father of the child. The 1874 Births and Death Registration Act closed this loophole, and from then on the father of an illegitimate child had to be present at the registration in order for his name to appear.

- *Name, surname and maiden surname of mother*

Along with the family's address, the mother's maiden surname is probably the most useful piece of information that you'll find on a birth certificate, as it provides a link to the parents' marriage certificate. In most cases the details will be entered something like:

Mary Smith
formerly Jones

indicating that Mary's maiden surname was Jones.

Things start to get a bit more difficult if the mother had been married before. Then you might get an entry like:

Mary Smith,
late Brown
formerly Jones

which tells us that Mary was born as Mary Jones, was previously married to someone called Brown, but is now married to Mr Smith.

In the case of an illegitimate birth, whether a father's name is given or not, the unmarried mother would normally appear as Mary Jones, with no other surnames mentioned. Unless, of course, it was an illegitimate birth to a married woman, in which case you might need to speak to an expert to get the correct interpretation –these things can get very complicated!

You should also bear in mind that there was nothing – other than their own sense of right or wrong – to stop an unmarried couple claiming to be married when registering a birth. The information given to the registrars was taken on trust and there was no requirement to produce a marriage certificate as evidence.

• *Occupation of father*

This column offers very little scope for misunderstanding, confusion or ambiguity; if a father is shown on the certificate, his occupation will be entered here. There may be a temptation to exaggerate his status, but in most cases what you see is what you get.

- *Signature, description and residence of informant*

This is a very important piece of information which is often overlooked. The informant was usually the child's mother (most working fathers wouldn't have been able to take the time off to register a birth), but occasionally you'll find the name of a relative who lived where the child was born (an aunt or a grandparent), and from 1875 onwards anyone who was present at the birth could act as the informant. If the informant was illiterate, then rather than a signature you will see the words 'the mark of ...' together with an 'X'. Pay close attention to this, as an illiterate ancestor wouldn't have been able to check that the details they had given had been recorded accurately.

In most cases, the informant's residence will be the same as the place of birth, but sometimes a more detailed address is given. If the address in this column is completely different from the one in the 'where born' column, then you'll need to investigate the birthplace address. It may be the address of a relative – a grandparent, for example – but it could equally turn out to be a hospital or workhouse.

- *When registered and signature of registrar*

These columns contain little of value to family historians except that the date of registration determines which quarterly index will list the birth. The registration should occur within six weeks of the date of birth, and penalties were in place for late registration. If a birth was registered late, the certificate had to be countersigned by the Superintendent Registrar.

- *Name entered after registration*

This column is usually left blank, but in those rare cases when a child was registered before being named there is the provision to register the name up to a year after the birth. Christian names added at baptism can also be entered here.

Changes in 1969

On 1 April 1969 a completely new format was introduced for birth certificates and is still in use today. The place of birth of both parents is now shown on all English and Welsh birth certificates – if only this information had been recorded from the start! – and the mother's occupation is usually given, but otherwise the details are exactly the same as on earlier certificates.

Searching for a birth certificate

In order to carry out an effective search for a birth certificate in the GRO indexes, you need to know a certain amount of information about the person whose birth you're looking for, and there are a number of points you need to consider, as illustrated in the checklist on pages 42–3.

Non-registration of births

In the early years there was a certain amount of resistance to the whole idea of civil registration, and we know that from the late 1830s right up to the early 1900s a small but significant percentage of events went unregistered. This was largely a problem with births, and some parts of England and Wales seem to have been affected more than others. In 1875, the responsibility for ensuring that births were registered was transferred from the registrars to the parents, but this change doesn't seem to have had any significant effect. Research has shown that the number of births registered each year increased steadily throughout the 1870s without any sign of a surge in 1875.

So, if your search for a birth certificate is unsuccessful it is *possible* that the birth was never registered, but it's far more likely that some of the 'facts' that you know about the birth are wrong. Perhaps the person was a year or two older than you had been led to believe. Their surname may have been spelt in an unexpected way or they may even have been registered under a completely different name – their mother's maiden surname, for example.

There are a number of options to consider before giving up and assuming that your ancestor's birth wasn't registered.

Linking GRO certificates to census returns

We'll deal with census returns in some detail in Chapter 4 but at this stage it's worth looking at how birth, marriage and death certificates, and census returns are related to each other.

As well as being responsible for the civil registration process, the General Register Office was in charge of taking the censuses. In order to do this as efficiently as possible, the system of registration districts and sub-districts used for registering births, marriages and deaths was also used to compile the census returns. Among other things, this enabled the GRO to compare birth rates with population change in different areas.

Checklist: birth certificate searches

Do you know their full name (including any middle names)?

- *People often used a different name to the one they were born with.*
- *Nicknames such as Jack or Bill can disguise a more 'correct' name.*
- *A distinctive middle name can help to identify a person's birth, but people were not always consistent about using middle names – even in official documents.*
- *The surname could be spelt in an unexpected way – standard spelling of names is a relatively modern phenomenon.*
- *The birth could have been registered under the mother's maiden name if the parents weren't actually married.*

Do you know when they were born?

- *What is the source of this information?*
- *Remember that family memories can be flawed – the day and month are more likely to be accurate than the year.*

- *Do you know how old they were when they were married?*
- *Do you know how old they were when they died?*
- *Do you have their age from a census return?*
- *Do these ages 'match'?*
- *Remember that information from documents can be inaccurate – the more sources you've looked at, the more likely you are to have an accurate date of birth.*

Do you know where they were born?

- *What is the source of this information?*
- *Do you have their place of birth from a census return?*
- *Don't forget that information from documents can be inaccurate – you may find a different place of birth given in a different census year.*
- *Do you know which registration district covers the place where they were born? Remember that it is the registration district that will appear in the index.*

Did you know?
The first four national census returns, taken in 1801, 1811, 1821 and 1831, were simply headcounts, and no official records were made of individual names. However, some conscientious enumerators made lists of the inhabitants in their areas and a small number of these lists have survived. They are usually found in the relevant county record office.

The details that you find on your ancestors' birth and death certificates, in particular the names of the registration district and sub-district, provide a direct link to the census and can easily be used to find the returns for the family's address. The census returns for a particular address shown on a birth certificate will always appear in the contemporary returns for the registration district and sub-district that are shown on the certificate.

Adoptions

In 1926 the General Register Office began to register adoptions. Before this date there was no legal adoption process and children could be adopted informally, without any official record being made of the event. Unless the child kept their birth surname, it can be almost impossible to trace their origins.

The Adopted Children's Register contains a record of all adoptions in England and Wales since 1 January 1926. An index is available at the Family Records Centre in London, and adoption certificates can be ordered there in person or from the General Register Office in Southport. However, you should note that there is nothing, either in the indexes or on the adoption certificates themselves, which will enable you to identify the birth certificate of the adopted child. The child's date of birth is given, but unless the child was adopted under the same name that they were given at birth this will not really help you.

The whole process of adoption is a very sensitive matter. The Adopted Children's Register is not designed to meet the needs of family historians and the General Register Office are currently looking at ways of restricting access to adoption records so that only those who really need to use the records will be able to do so.

Piecing together a life

It's important to understand right from the start that the documents we use in researching our family history were not designed with genealogists in mind. Birth, marriage and death certificates, census returns, parish registers, wills and other legal records were created for their own distinct purposes, and we should look on it as very fortunate that they have survived and that they are available for us to consult today. The way in which these records were compiled means that they are not necessarily arranged in the best way for family historians to use; the census returns, for example, are arranged by address rather than by name.

One of the main attractions of family history is the opportunity it offers to ordinary people to carry out original historical research. And for the majority of the population without any familiarity with this sort of research, setting out on the trail of discovery can be a unique, exciting and, at times, daunting experience. This is our chance to find out about events that took place centuries ago, to solve mysteries that have lain unsolved for years on end, to investigate how our ancestors lived and how their lives were influenced by the major events of the day.

To do all this we need to start thinking like detectives. The documents that we use are not explicitly linked – the information that you find on a marriage certificate may help you to identify the record of the bride's birth, but nothing on the certificate will unequivocally identify the correct birth certificate for her. There is no 'life record' that brings together, on one document, the details of an individual's life. So it's up to us to create our own life records – to make the links between the various sources we use in our research – and we therefore need to be able to look at the documents with a critical eye and consider what it is they're telling us about our ancestors. We need to understand how the information we find on one document will lead us to another source and how to interpret the details that the records reveal.

CERTIFIED COPY OF AN ENTRY OF MARRIAGE

GIVEN AT THE GENERAL REGISTER OFFICE

Application Number PRO2001

1839. Marriage solemnized at the Parish Church in the Parish of Maer in the County of Stafford

No.	When Married	Name and Surname	Age	Condition	Rank or Profession	Residence at the Time of Marriage	Father's Name and Surname	Rank or Profession of Father
275	Jan 29 1839	Charles Robert Darwin	Of full age	Bachelor	Esquire	Mill Lane	Robert Waring Darwin	Doctor
		Emma Wedgwood	Of full age	Spinster		Maer	Josiah Wedgwood	Esquire

Married in the Parish Church according to the Rites and Ceremonies of the Established Church by me

This Marriage was solemnized between us { Charles Robert Darwin / Emma Wedgwood }   in the Presence of us { Josiah Wedgwood / Caroline Elizabeth Wedgwood }

CERTIFIED to be a true copy of an entry in the certified copy of a register of Marriages in the Registration District of **Newcastle under Lyme**

Given at the GENERAL REGISTER OFFICE, under the Seal of the said Office, the **5th** day of **February 2001**

MXA 762754

A certified copy of the marriage certificate of Charles Darwin and Emma Wodehouse, 29 January 1839. As here, marriage witnesses are often relatives.

Chapter 3

Coming together: marriage records

Marriage certificates

It would be almost impossible to carry out serious family history research without using marriage certificates at some time. The information on these certificates provides a vital bridge between generations and can open up whole new areas of research. Marriage certificates can also be quite difficult to interpret and can offer a number of traps for the unwary.

The introduction of civil marriages in 1837 was one of the most contentious aspects of a surprisingly controversial Act of Parliament. At the time of the Act, the established Church of England still wielded enormous power, particularly through the role of the bishops in the House of Lords, and they were successful in overturning several of the original proposals in the Bill, including one to introduce civil ceremonies for all marriages. There was great resistance to the whole idea of the Church losing its exclusive role in this area, and the influence of the bishops is reflected in many of the terms of the Act as it was eventually passed. For example, even though nonconformist chapels could now be licensed for marriages, it wasn't until the 1898 Authorized Persons Act was passed that ministers could perform ceremonies without a registrar having to be present – and even then, each minister had to apply to become an 'authorized person'.

Copies of marriage certificates and also the indexes to them are available from the places that were mentioned in Chapter 2, and all of the online resources listed are equally useful in searching for marriages. But with most marriages an alternative and potentially cheaper source is also available. If your Victorian ancestors were married in a church or chapel, it is highly likely that the register has been deposited in the relevant county record office, where it can be consulted (usually on microfilm) for free. Of course, the problem is knowing which church they were married in (the GRO's indexes won't tell you that), and if they married in a register office the records won't have been deposited; but if you've got more time than money on your hands, this option might be worth considering.

The GRO's indexes to marriages show the following details for each entry:

- name
- surname of spouse (from MAR 1912)
- registration district
- reference number (volume and page)

The entries for the bride and the groom will always have the same reference number, so if you know the full names of both parties you can easily cross-reference them to ensure that you've found the right marriage. Even in the years before each index entry included the spouse's surname, both names should be entered.

The layout of the certificates is still the same today as it was on 1 July 1837 when marriages were first registered by the General Register Office. Each certificate shows the registration district, the date and place of the marriage and the following information about the bride and the groom:

- when married
- name and surname
- age
- condition
- rank or profession
- residence at the time of marriage
- father's name and surname
- father's rank or profession

At the bottom of the form you will find the signatures of the couple, two or more witnesses and the officiating minister or registrar, as well as information about the wedding itself – the religious denomination and whether the marriage was by licence, by certificate or after banns.

Let's look at these areas in more detail:

- *When married*

This is usually pretty straightforward. Sometimes the year isn't given here but it should always appear at the top of the form.

- *Name and surname*

The names of both parties (usually, but not always, including any middle names) are entered here. In the case of a widow remarrying, her former married name rather than her maiden name should be given – you'll get her maiden surname from her father's name.

- *Age*

Frustratingly, the age is often given simply as 'Of full age', meaning that the person was 21 years or over. The good news is that, although this practice was fairly common in the early years of registration, it died out long before the end of the 19th century, and you can consider yourself unfortunate if you come across it much after the 1870s.

- *Condition*

The marital status of both parties will be recorded here. You're most likely to find the terms

'Bachelor', 'Spinster', 'Widower' and 'Widow', although you may also stumble on the occasional 'Divorcee'.

- *Rank or profession*

The occupation of both parties is entered here, but more often than not there will be a line or a blank space where the bride's rank or profession would appear.

- *Residence at the time of marriage*

Compared to the addresses given on birth and death certificates, the information in this section is of relatively little use to family historians. The addresses given are frequently imprecise or simply inaccurate (see below for more on this topic).

- *Father's name and surname*

This is occasionally left blank, which would normally indicate illegitimacy, but it is not unknown for a deceased father's name to be omitted.

- *Father's rank or profession*

The groom's and bride's fathers' occupations are entered here.

It's easy to see how useful marriage certificates are. They give you a direct link from one generation to another, and the ages of the bride and groom, combined with their fathers' names, can help you to identify records of their births. You can also learn about your ancestors' religious persuasion; a marriage in a Baptist chapel could lead to the discovery of a long tradition of nonconformity in the family.

However, marriage certificates can also be the most frustrating of documents to work with. The problem is that all the information supplied by the bride and groom was taken on trust by the clerk or the registrar and very rarely questioned, yet there are any number of reasons why the couple may have chosen to be 'economical with the truth'.

Of the three major life events that are recorded by the GRO, marriages are the only ones where you provide the information yourself: your birth is usually registered by one of your parents and your death by your next of kin, but with a marriage you're the one supplying the details. And whereas births and deaths are registered in private, the marriage register is signed publicly in front of the minister or registrar as well as two or more witnesses. There are also a number of restrictions regarding marriage, most notably age, marital status and relationship to a chosen partner.

All of this presents a determined couple with

the temptation to tell a few half-truths, untruths or even downright lies in order to get married without too many difficult questions being asked. Technically, anyone doing so was guilty of perjury, but you'd be amazed to find out how many of our ancestors lied – and got away with it.

And it's easy to see how this can cause problems when it comes to understanding what the certificate is telling you. The first and most common problem you might encounter is with the ages of the bride and groom. Children under the age of 21 needed their parents' consent in order to marry, but since there was no requirement to produce evidence of age and it was very rarely checked by the person performing the ceremony, it was quite easy for a 19-year-old to claim to be 21 or 'of full age'. An older woman marrying a younger man might knock a few years off her age, and where there was a substantial age difference between the couple there was often a tendency to 'narrow the gap'. For example a 40-year-old man marrying a woman of 25 might be recorded in the register as 35 and 30 respectively. And remember that 'of full age' doesn't mean 21 years old or even 'over 21', as some people seem to believe: it actually means '21 years old *or more*'. A 62-year-old could as easily be described as 'of full age' as a 22-year-old.

The marital condition can also present problems. At a time when divorce was not a realistic option for most ordinary people, it was simpler for a man wanting to remarry while his 'first' wife was still alive to declare himself to be either a bachelor or a widower. As long as he was marrying in an area where he wasn't known, it was unlikely that anyone would ever find out. However, bigamy was considered a very serious crime and many people were prosecuted.

Addresses on marriage certificates are notoriously imprecise or even inaccurate. Marriages taking place within the Church of England had to be performed either by licence or after the calling of banns. The process of marrying by banns was by far the cheaper of the two options, but first there were a few hurdles to jump. Banns had to be called in the parish church for three successive weeks preceding the date of the ceremony, allowing people who might know of a reason why the couple were not legally allowed to marry to make an objection – there are numerous examples of the bride's father forbidding the banns on the second or third week of calling! If the couple came from two different parishes, the banns would be called in both.

The parties also had to be resident in the parish for at least a week before the banns were called. In practice, this was a difficult rule to enforce – after all, residency was not an easy thing to prove one way or another – and for this reason the address given on a marriage certificate is often no more than an address of convenience. It may have been a temporary lodging or it may have been the residence of one of the witnesses, but there's a distinct possibility that your ancestor never actually lived there. Alarm bells should certainly start to ring when you find the same address given for the bride and the groom. It is unlikely that they lived together (in the modern sense of the phrase) before getting married, although the groom may have been a lodger in the bride's house – and again, it's possible that they had both simply given an address of convenience in order to meet the residency requirements.

Another area which causes a great deal of difficulty on marriage certificates surrounds the fathers' details. There are two potential stumbling blocks here; first, there's the problem that confronts you when you come across a big blank space where the father's name should be. As mentioned before, this usually indicates that the person marrying was illegitimate, but as always with marriage certificates, it's not as simple as that. In the 19th century there was a very real stigma attached to illegitimacy. Despite the fact

Did you know?
Hardwicke's Marriage Act was passed in 1753 and came into effect the following year. This Act is particularly important for family historians. It outlawed clandestine marriages and meant that the vast majority of marriages in England and Wales between 1754 and 1837 took place in Church of England parish churches. Only Jews and Quakers were exempt from the terms of the Act.

that a fairly sizeable percentage of the population was illegitimate, it wasn't something that was discussed openly or readily admitted to. So when an illegitimate person went to church to get married there was a strong temptation to invent a father – usually conveniently deceased.

And that brings us on to the other main area of confusion regarding the fathers' details. None of the various Marriage Acts carried an explicit instruction to indicate whether the fathers of the bride and groom were dead or alive at the time of the wedding. Some clerks did so, by entering the word 'deceased' in brackets after the father's name, but many didn't, and it's this inconsistency that can lead you to misinterpret the information that you're presented with: because the absence of the word 'deceased' does not necessarily mean that the father was still alive. The rule of thumb here is that if neither father is described as deceased you should assume in the first place (and until you find evidence to the contrary) that both are still alive. If one of the fathers is described as deceased, it's fairly safe to assume that the other one is alive, while if both are shown to be deceased they probably were – although you can't rule out wishful thinking on the part of the bride or groom. And don't forget the possibility, mentioned above, that the 'deceased' father was actually fictitious.

Fathers' occupations were often exaggerated on marriage certificates, so don't take them too literally.

As with the signatures on birth certificates, watch out for people making their marks – an indication of illiteracy. And bear in mind that if you were unable to read and write you would also be unable to check what the clerk had written for accuracy.

Two witnesses were required to testify to the accuracy of the information supplied and to confirm that there was no 'lawful impediment' preventing the couple from marrying. Although they were usually relatives or friends of the couple it's not uncommon to find that 'professional' witnesses were employed. A shilling or two would secure the services of a churchwarden if there were no relatives on hand.

The best advice is to use the information that you get from marriage certificates with extreme caution. It may be reliable and it may not. It's only by comparing the details with information from other sources that we can untangle the web of deceit that some of our ancestors left behind.

Searching for a marriage certificate

Searching for a marriage certificate in the GRO indexes can be a difficult process. One of the first things to consider is which of the two names you're going to search under. It might seem obvious to look for the less common of the two, but if the surname is very uncommon there's a chance that it has been spelt incorrectly so you might want to try the more common name instead. It doesn't really matter which you choose as the marriage should be indexed under the names of both parties.

Checklist: marriage certificate searches

Do you know their full names (including any middle names)?

- *People often used a different name to the one they were born with.*
- *One or both of the surnames could be spelt in an unexpected way – standard spelling of names is a relatively modern phenomenon.*

Do you know where they were married?

- *What is the source of this information? Remember that family memories can be flawed!*
- *Do you know how old they were when they were married?*
- *Do you know when their first child was born?*
- *Marriage under the age of 17 was extremely rare – most people married in their early to mid twenties.*

Do you know where they were born?

- *What is the source of this information?*
- *Do you know where their first child was born?*
- *Do you know where the bride came from? A large proportion of marriages took place in the bride's 'home' parish.*
- *Do you know which registration district covers the place where they were married? Remember that it is the registration district that will appear in the index.*

Asking the right questions

The first task you should undertake when you get hold of a new document is to ask yourself whether there can be any doubt that you have the right one. If, for example, you've just got a copy of a birth certificate which you are hoping relates to your ancestor, have a look at the father's occupation and check that it matches what you already know about him. If you were expecting a merchant banker and what you've got in your hands is a bricklayer, then it's probably not the right certificate. Of course, some people did change jobs during their lives, but a tradesman or an artisan is unlikely to become an agricultural labourer in later life and you wouldn't expect a clerk to end up working down a mine.

Only when you've proved beyond any reasonable doubt that the document is 'yours' can you start planning the next stage of your research.

We've already seen how important it is to question the 'facts' supplied by your relatives, and you'll soon find out that it's also your job as a family history detective to question the accuracy of the information on the documents you uncover. It's impossible to quantify the extent of the problem, but it's certainly true to say that a fairly substantial percentage of the birth, marriage and death certificates and the censuses that you'll look at in the course of your research will contain information that is, to some degree, inaccurate.

There are a number of quite separate reasons for this. First, there's the whole range of problems brought about by illiteracy and regional accents, which we'll look at in more detail in Chapter 4. You also need to bear in mind that, when you order a certificate, what you're getting is a *copy* of a copy of the original. The registrar may have recorded the details accurately at the time the event was registered, but it's quite easy to see how mistakes can creep in when the quarterly returns are sent to the General Register Office. However thorough the clerk was, however meticulously he transcribed the details from the registers, he was after all only human and as prone to error as the rest of us.

We've already touched on the next cause of inaccuracy on our ancestors' documents, and it's probably the most significant one. Whether we like it or not, the fact of the matter is that our ancestors had all manner of reasons why they might not be entirely truthful when it came to completing census forms and registering births, marriages and deaths.

The final point to consider here is that our ancestors might simply not have known the 'truth'. A person who didn't know where they were born might have found it easier to invent a place of birth than to admit his ignorance when the census enumerator came calling.

If the information you've got is accurate then your research will be that much easier and more straightforward, but if things start not to add up, if you're failing to find your ancestors where you'd expect to find them, then you need to start asking yourself some questions. 'Could my ancestor have been lying about his age when he got married? Was he really born in Birmingham? His marriage certificate indicates that his father was called John, but could this be a mistake for Joseph?' The best way to tackle these problems is to find as many records of your ancestors as possible. Try to find them in each of the census returns to see if any of the details are different or simply clearer, and don't forget the possibility of a second marriage and the information you could get there.

But whatever else you do, keep asking the right questions!

The census return for Charles Darwin's home at Downe House, Downe, Kent, 1881. Family, servants and visitors are all shown.

Chapter 4

Counting the people: census returns

- The dates of the censuses
- The 1841 census
- The 1851 to 1901 censuses
- Viewing the censuses
- Finding your ancestors in the census returns

In 1801 an event took place which has had an enormous impact on family historians. This was the year when the first national census was taken, and every ten years since then (apart from 1941 when the country was occupied with other matters) the process has been repeated.

There has always been a degree of suspicion about why the government was asking all these questions, and in order to encourage people to give the information certain guarantees were given about the confidentiality of the census returns. The result of this is that the returns are 'closed' for a hundred years and the 1901 census is therefore currently the latest available.

The census forms themselves contain some of the most valuable information that family historians will ever come across – it's almost as if they were created with us in mind. But the real purpose of the censuses has always been to enable the government of the day to understand what was happening to the population and to assist with long-term planning of public services and expenditure. The returns from the 19th century record the dramatic change in Britain from a predominantly rural society in 1801 to a heavily urbanized one a hundred years later.

It's the arrangement of the censuses that makes them so useful. A schedule was delivered

The dates of the censuses

1801	10 March
1811	27 May
1821	28 May
1831	29 May
1841	6 June
1851	30 March
1861	7 April
1871	2 April
1881	3 April
1891	5 April
1901	31 March

to each household a few days before census day (which was always a Sunday) and the completed forms were collected on the following Monday. The details were then copied into the census books by the enumerators. The returns for each household record the names and certain other details of every person who was present there on the night of the census and, crucially for our purposes, they show how the various members of the household were related to each other.

However, the first censuses were simply head-counts, and it wasn't until the fifth decennial census was taken in 1841 that the government started to ask for this detailed information about individuals. The official returns from the first four censuses were destroyed after the statistical information had been taken from them, but some of the enumerators compiled lists of the names of the people living in their districts and a small number of these lists have survived. If you're very lucky you might just find a pre-1841 census for the parish where your ancestors lived.

The 1841 census

The 1841 census is, therefore, effectively the first of the 19th-century censuses, but even this doesn't give us a huge amount of information about our ancestors. The schedules record details for each household under the following headings:

- NAMES of each Person who abode therein the preceding Night
- AGE and SEX:
  – Males
  – Females
- PROFESSION, TRADE, EMPLOYMENT or of INDEPENDENT MEANS:
  – Where Born
  – Whether Born in same County
  – Whether Born in Scotland, Ireland or Foreign Parts

The address of each household is also given, although this is often no more than the name of the village, and house numbers are rarely shown. Middle names are not entered as a rule, but it's the age columns in 1841 which lead to the greatest confusion. The instructions to the enumerators were to round down the ages of all people aged over 15 to the nearest five years. Therefore, anyone aged between 20 and 24 should appear in the 1841 census as 20, and a 72-year-old would be entered as 70. This rule wasn't always strictly applied and it's not uncommon to find the precise ages of adults, but you need to be careful with how you interpret the information in these columns.

There's not a lot of room on the forms for the occupations and they do tend to be quite vague and imprecise. They are also often heavily contracted so you should make sure that you're familiar with some of the most common abbreviations:

Ag Lab (or AL)	Agricultural labourer
MS	Male servant
FS	Female servant
Ind	Independent – i.e. 'of independent means'
Ap	Apprentice
Shoe m	Shoemaker

The last two columns relate to the individual's place of birth, and the information here is unfortunately not very useful for our purposes. In the majority of cases all you get is a 'Y' (for Yes) in the column headed 'Whether Born in same County' and all this tells you is that your ancestor was born in the county in which they are currently living – it's not a lot to go on and it's also frequently inaccurate. It's even more frustrating to find an 'N' in this column, as this suggests that your ancestor was born in another county but gives you no clue as to which one!

The 1851 to 1901 censuses

The questions asked in the later censuses, from 1851 right up to 1901, are almost identical as far as the information relating to our ancestors is concerned. There was a gradual increase in the amount of detail that was requested concerning the buildings that our ancestors lived in, and new questions regarding employment status and mental and physical health were introduced over the years, but the basic structure and layout of the census page remained the same throughout the whole of this period.

At the top of the page there was a series of boxes that identified the locality. In 1851 this included the names of the parish or township, ecclesiastical district, city or borough, town and village. By the end of the century, the number of boxes had increased to eight:

- administrative county
- civil parish
- ecclesiastical parish
- county borough, municipal borough or urban district
- ward of municipal borough or urban district;
- rural district
- parliamentary borough or division
- town or village or hamlet

This information shouldn't be ignored as it all helps to gain a better understanding of the sort of area that your ancestors lived in.

The rest of the census page was divided into a number of columns in which the enumerator entered the details of each household and, more importantly for us, recorded some illuminating facts about our ancestors. In each of the censuses from 1851 to 1901, the following information was recorded about each person:

- name and surname
- relation to head of family
- marital condition

- age
- profession or occupation
- where born

It's easy to see how enormously useful this information can be, particularly when your ancestors are so conveniently packaged together in family groups. The name, age and place of birth of an individual provide you with all the information you need to carry out an effective search for their birth certificate, and if you're looking for a marriage, the age of the oldest child should help you to determine when the event is likely to have taken place.

But the censuses are no different to any other documentary evidence that our ancestors left behind and, as we've already seen with marriage certificates, there are a number of reasons why the information may be inaccurate. The very process by which the census was taken presents ample opportunity for mistakes to creep in. The high level of illiteracy in the 19th century meant that many householders were unable to complete the census schedules themselves. In these cases, the enumerator would ask the questions and note down what he heard; this could lead to all sorts of problems with unusual names – both personal names and place names – particularly if

Did you know?

From 1851 onwards, the census was taken either at the end of March or at the beginning of April. It's important to know this when you're trying to calculate your ancestors' dates of birth. If someone's age was given as 7 at the time of the 1861 census, don't assume that they were born in 1854 – in fact they would have been born sometime between April 1853 and March 1854.

the householder had a strong regional accent which was unfamiliar to the enumerator.

Ages on census returns are frequently inaccurate and need to be treated with extreme caution – there are countless examples of people ageing substantially more, or a lot less, than ten years between censuses! Whether this is most likely to be due to the householder's ignorance, a deliberate attempt to deceive or an error by the enumerator it's difficult to say, but you should never rely on the age being accurate until you've checked it against other sources.

The 'where born' column can throw up just as many problems and can lead to the same sort of difficulties when tracing birth certificates. Something to watch out for here is that people tend to be less precise about their birthplace the further away from it they are. For example, a person born in Moseley in Staffordshire but living in

London might say that they were born in Wolverhampton (the nearest large town), and if they were living in the West Midlands they might give their place of birth as Wednesfield (the parish which includes Moseley), but only if they were living in the Wednesfield area itself would they actually specify Moseley as their birthplace. Another problem (although admittedly not a very common one) is that some people simply didn't know where they were born, and it can be very frustrating to find the letters NK (for 'not known') entered where the place of birth should be.

In 1891 and 1901, census returns in Wales asked an additional question concerning the language spoken by each person: Welsh, English or both. In 1901, a similar question was asked on the Isle of Man regarding the Manx language.

Viewing the censuses

The only complete set of census returns for England and Wales (including the Channel Islands and the Isle of Man) is held by the Family Records Centre in London. Local and county record offices usually hold the returns for their own areas of interest, and the Latter-day Saints' worldwide network of family history centres can give you access to the returns for any area, although the microfilms will need to be ordered (for a small fee).

Perhaps the biggest advance in family history research in recent years has been the advent of websites providing online access to census returns. Within a year or so, all of the surviving returns for England and Wales from 1841 to 1901 will be accessible worldwide, 24 hours a day. And the good news is that they are fully indexed by name – so that, in theory at least, you should be able to find all of your ancestors wherever they were living. At the time of writing, the returns for 1901, 1891, 1881, 1871 and 1861 are available, with 1851 due to arrive in 2005, and 1841 in 2006.

The best way to access these online resources is to use the links on the National Archives' website at:

www.nationalarchives.gov.uk/census.

There is a charge to view the census pages, but this is a small price to pay for such unprecedented access to these invaluable documents.

Finding your ancestors in the census returns

You should always attempt to find your ancestors in each of the censuses – partly to 'iron out' any problems with ages and places of birth, but also because you just never know what will turn up. The elderly aunt staying with the family, the distant cousin from Cornwall or the previously unknown child who must have died young can all add to the story of your family and could even open up new areas for further research.

While it's clearly true that the recent advances in online access to the censuses have simplified the process of finding people in the returns, the indexes are known to contain errors and you'll sometimes find that you just can't track down the person you're looking for. So there will always be a need to understand how to search the censuses in the old-fashioned way.

Assuming that you're not using an online index (or that there isn't one for the census year you're interested in) it's worth investigating whether a local index has been compiled. Family history societies have been busily producing these indexes for the past thirty years or so and you might find that there's one covering your town or village. There are even indexes covering whole counties, often published on CDs.

If there isn't a name index, you'll have to get into the census by looking for your family at a particular address. The best way to do this is to use an address that you've found on a birth or death certificate, and since the census returns were arranged by address this should be a relatively straightforward process. We've already looked at the strong links between GRO certificates and census returns – remember that the same system of registration districts and sub-districts was used for both. If the birth was registered close to the date of the census, you've got a good chance of finding the family. However, people tended to move house quite frequently, particularly those living in rented accommodation in the heavily populated urban areas – the midnight flit when the rent was due seems to have been a fairly common event! So you shouldn't be too surprised if you don't find your ancestors where you expect them to be living, even a day or two before or after the family birth or death.

In order to carry out an effective search in the census returns you will need to have a certain amount of information about the person or family that you're looking for. If they were in a large town or city, you really need to have a good idea of where they were living – ideally, you should have a precise address from a birth or death certificate, a will or a trade directory.

Searching in a rural area is much easier, but you need to consider the possibility that your ancestors may have moved to a neighbouring parish. Most people didn't move more than about twenty miles from their birthplace (many spent their whole lives in the same village) so if you don't find the family where you're expecting to, a sweep of the surrounding area is always worthwhile.

There are also some important points to consider when searching for people in any of the online sources:

- If you don't find your family straight away, try to think about how the names could have been misinterpreted or mistranscribed by the indexers.
- Use wildcards – special characters such as * and ? – to find variant spellings.
- Don't be tempted to fill in all the boxes – if you enter too much information you will restrict your search too much and you run the risk of eliminating the entry you're looking for; the moral is 'less is more'.

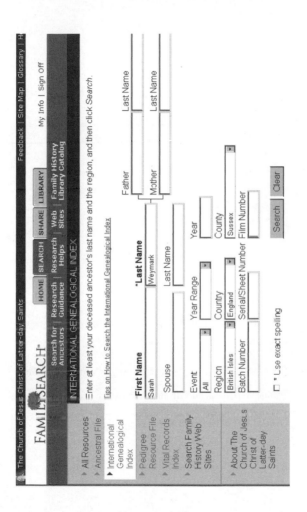

The International Genealogical Index search page as featured on the FamilySearch website www.familysearch.org

The name game

In Charles Dickens' classic novel *Great Expectations*, Pip, the hero of the story, asks his brother-in-law Joe Gargery how he spells his surname, to which Joe replies: 'I don't spell it at all.' And this exchange tells us all we need to know about standards of literacy in Victorian England. The fact of the matter is that the vast majority of the population couldn't read or write, and it wasn't until the Education Act of 1870 that the situation began to change and a degree of basic literacy became the norm.

Until then, the spelling of surnames and place names on census returns, GRO certificates and other documents we use, was only really of importance to the clerks who wrote the documents. If there's one lesson you should learn about family history research, it is to throw away the idea of a 'correct' way to spell your name. Names can and do get corrupted and altered over the years – take the surname SHAKESPEARE, for example. Here are just a few variations you might come across:

SHAKESPEAR   SHAXSPERE   SHAKESPIEAR
SHAKYSPERE   SHAKSPEARE   SHAKESPURRE
SHACKSPERE

And none of these is any more 'correct' than any of the others. There is no right or wrong - they are simply examples of how a clerk might interpret what he heard. And this can become even more complicated when you throw regional accents into the mix.

Take the case of your illiterate ancestor moving from Yorkshire to London and then being called upon to register the birth of his child. You can imagine how easy it would be for the registrar to get one or two details wrong. Or consider the family that moved from Somerset to Durham and, when it came to census time, told the enumerator that they were born in Crewkerne. You can easily forgive the enumerator for writing down Crooken in his book! Another common error to look out for is the dropped 'H' at the start of the name — HORWOOD can easily become ORWOOD — and the other side of the coin is that you may find an over-zealous clerk might add an 'H' wrongly, assuming that one had been dropped.

It's important to keep an open mind here and make sure that you stop yourself from saying 'But that's not how my name is spelt!' Remember that the whole concept of standard spellings of names is a relatively modern phenomenon.

You should think carefully about how your surname might have been spelt in the past. Even very common names like SMITH and BROWN can be prone to different spellings (SMYTH, SMITHE, BROWNE, BROUN, etc.) and the more uncommon your name is, the greater the chance that it has experienced a variety of spellings over the centuries.

A certified copy of the death certificate of Charles Darwin, 19 April 1882. Cause of death: 'angina'.

Chapter 5

Ashes to ashes: death records

Death certificates

Death certificates are often overlooked as a source for family historians, or at best they are undervalued. It's true to say that there is less information on a death certificate of an obviously genealogical nature than you would expect to find on birth or marriage certificates, but they certainly shouldn't be ignored.

Tracing records of deaths can be a frustrating and sometimes quite difficult process – particularly as the GRO's indexes didn't include ages until 1866. Before then, they showed only the following information:

- name
- registration district
- reference number (volume and page)

So if the person you're looking for had a name that was at all common, you might have real problems finding their death in this period. The deceased person's age is shown from 1866 until 1969, from which year their date of birth is shown instead.

The layout of English and Welsh death certificates was the same from the start of registration in 1837 until 1969. As with the birth certificates of the same period, the details were entered into a number of headed columns:

- when and where died
- name and surname
- sex
- age
- occupation
- cause of death
- signature, description and residence of informant
- when registered
- signature of registrar

Again, we need to have a look at each of these headings in more detail.

- *When and where died*

The place of death will normally be the deceased person's home address, but many people died in workhouses or hospitals some distance from where they lived. Crucially for our purposes, these institutions may have been situated in a completely different registration district, and since deaths are always registered in the district in which they occur this might complicate the search for your ancestor's death. This is mainly a problem in London, with its physically small but densely populated registration districts, but even in rural areas it's a problem that you might occasionally come up against. And don't overlook the possibility that your ancestor may have died suddenly either at work or while travelling.

• *Name and surname*

Married women and widows will be listed under their married names – i.e. their husband's surname. If they had been married more than once, only the latest surname will be shown.

• *Sex*

The single word 'Male' or 'Female' should be entered here.

• *Age*

The information here is normally pretty reliable, but bear in mind that the informant (see below) may not have known the deceased very well.

• *Occupation*

This is a rather misleading heading and the information recorded here is not always what you might expect. If the deceased was an adult male then his occupation will be entered, but if the deceased was a woman or a child then it can start to get quite complicated.

Children will normally be described as the '*son of ...*' or the '*daughter of ...*' and married or widowed women as the '*wife of ...*' or the

Did you know?

As part of her campaign to raise awareness of the effects of poor housing and unsanitary living conditions on the health of the population, Florence Nightingale asked the GRO to include questions on the 1861 census that would provide her with statistical data. In a letter to William Farr she wrote, 'We should have a return of the whole sick and diseases in the United Kingdom for one spring day which would give a good average idea of the sanitary state of all classes of the population.' Her request was not met.

'*widow of ...*' followed in each case by the name of their father or husband and *his* occupation.

The situation with unmarried women is even more confusing and you may come across any one of a number of possibilities. An occupation might be given, but more often than not you'll find the words '*daughter of ...*' together with the father's name and occupation. There could even be a blank space or a line through the box. An interesting example of the rather confused thinking behind all this is the case of Florence Nightingale, who died in 1910 at the age of 90. Her death certificate describes her as the daughter of William Edward Nightingale – a man who had died some thirty-six years previously. There's a very strong case here for arguing that Florence could perhaps have been credited with having an occupation of her own!

- *Cause of death*

There are a couple of problems you might encounter here. First, before the implementation of the 1874 Registration Act, the cause of death tends to be a bit vague. Entries such as 'Old age' or 'Senile debility' are not at all uncommon, and when you come across 'Visitation from God' as a cause of death you do begin to wonder about the accuracy of the other details on the certificate.

Second, from 1875 death registrations had to be certified by a doctor, and from this point on a good dictionary will come in handy for interpreting the causes of death, which are normally given in their full medical form. Many of the diseases will be well known to us, such as cholera, typhus and bronchitis, but you may not have come across terms like 'syncope' (a faint caused by the heart stopping beating which could often result in death) and 'phthisis' (more familiar to us as that killer of young Victorian women, consumption or tuberculosis). The causes of death of our working-class urban ancestors can make for quite upsetting reading, but it all helps us to build up a better picture of the conditions they had to endure – and discovering these distressing aspects of their lives (and deaths) is just as important as learning about the good times.

- *Signature, description and residence of informant*

This may seem obvious, but the person whose death is being registered did *not* provide the details to the registrar! And the identity of the person who *did* provide the information is therefore quite crucial to us, as the reliability and accuracy of the information on the certificate is entirely dependent on how well that person knew the deceased. So, if the informant was the person's spouse, there's every reason to believe that the details are accurate; but if a neighbour performed the task you may want to ask some questions.

- *When registered*

From 1837 until 1874 all deaths had to be registered within eight days. This was then reduced to five days under the terms of an Act which tightened up and clarified several aspects of the original Birth and Deaths Registration Act of 1836. In practice, most deaths have always been registered within two or three days of the event.

If an inquest had taken place, particularly if the death was of a suspicious nature, then the registration could be delayed considerably. And remember that it's the date of registration which determines when the death will be entered in the GRO's indexes. Although the vast majority of deaths are registered in the same quarter as they occurred, you should never ignore the possibility that the entry will be found in the quarter following the date of death.

• *Signature of registrar*

Unless your ancestor was a registrar, this is unlikely to be of any significance to you!

• *Additional information*

From 1 April 1969, the deceased person's date and place of birth are shown on death certificates. Also from this date, the maiden surname of married or widowed women is recorded.

It's a good idea to get copies of as many death certificates as possible – at least for your direct ancestors – simply because you just don't know what you will find. Death certificates provide you with links to so many other sources (for example, wills, newspaper reports and burial or cemetery records) and if you're fortunate enough to discover an ancestor who died suddenly under mysterious or perhaps even grisly circumstances, then you could be in for a treat!

The clue here will be a reference to an inquest and, although it is probable that the actual record of the proceedings won't have survived, the chances are that there will have been a report in the local newspaper. Be warned that these reports can be quite graphic – there was nothing our Victorian ancestors liked more than reading about gruesome, horrific deaths at the breakfast table. And if there *is* a report, you are likely to get some invaluable biographical details that paint a picture of your ancestors and their daily lives which you simply won't be able to get from the usual official documents.

Searching for a death certificate

One of the most difficult aspects of finding the record of a death is to know where to start searching. With a birth or a marriage you can use ages and children's details from census returns to work out when the events were likely to have taken place, while the best you can hope for with a death is to use the 'disappearance' of a family member between one census and the next to narrow the search down to ten years at the most. The only alternative is to start with the last date when you know for certain that your ancestor was alive and begin your search from there. But

Checklist: death certificate searches

Do you know their full name (including any middle names)?

- *A person's death could be registered under a different name to the one by which they were commonly known.*
- *Married women and widows will be registered under their married name.*

Do you know when they died?

- *What is the source of this information?*
- *Details taken from tombstones can be inaccurate as they were often engraved many years after the event.*
- *Remember that dates provided by relatives may be no more than guesswork.*

you should be warned – you could be in for a long search.

Another approach to the problem might be to see if your ancestor left a will. Knowing when

Do you know where they died?

- *What is the source of this information?*
- *If someone died while they were away from home, their death would be registered in that place rather than their usual place of residence.*
- *Older people often moved to be close to their relatives.*

Do you know how old they were when they died?

- *What is the source of this information?*
- *Remember that ages from sources such as marriage certificates and census returns, and even the age recorded at death, can be inaccurate.*

their will was proved should lead you to a record of their death. We'll have a closer look at wills in the next chapter.

Get organized

Even if you decide at first to concentrate all your efforts on just one of your ancestral lines, you'll soon find that the amount of information you've gathered begins to get out of hand.

Those hastily scribbled notes you made on the back of an envelope during the phone call to Uncle Harold, that list of birth references you noted down on your last trip to the Family Records Centre, and the family group you found in the 1881 census are all vital pieces of evidence. But can you honestly say that you really have all the facts at your fingertips? Is the information organized in a way that makes it all easily accessible? You may not even realize that you have a problem until you're contacted by a distant cousin in Canada and you try to put together a clear and concise reply to her email, summarizing what you know about your bit of the family.

So you need to give careful consideration to how you are going to organize the results of your research. And there's no right or wrong way to go about it. Some people use paper filing systems with pre-printed forms to record what they know about each of their ancestors, some store their information on hundreds of index cards, while others use one of the many software packages specifically designed for the job. The important thing is to use a method that works for you. You need to be realistic about the amount of time you have to dedicate to what is after all (dare I say it?) simply a hobby. You certainly shouldn't let yourself become a slave to your system and find that keeping your notes properly organized is taking all the fun out of it.

Whether you're using a computer or a paper-based system you'll soon discover that creating a family tree or a pedigree is an excellent way of bringing all your facts together and illustrating the extent of your knowledge on a particular branch of the family. The tree doesn't have to be an ornate, highly decorative work of art – what's important is that it should be clear and easy to understand. A good family tree should also help you to plan future areas of research by showing gaps in your knowledge.

One good habit that you should get into right from the outset is to make a note of what sources you use in your research. Even if your search was unsuccessful, knowing that you have already looked for your family in the census returns for Little Sodbury will stop you from wasting your time repeating the search six months later. It's also good practice to make a note of your sources so that when you're telling a fellow researcher about a crucial detail relating to your ancestors, or asking for advice from a member of staff in a record office, you can explain how you came to know your 'facts'.

'The Last Will and Testament' of Charles Darwin (died 1882). It was accompanied by a grant of probate, naming executors.

Chapter 6

The will of the people: probate records

- Wills since 1858
- Wills before 1858
- Interpreting wills
- Administrations and inventories
- Death duty records
- Wills and probate: some useful terms

Whether your ancestors owned large swathes of land in the north of England or came from a more humble background in the West Country, the chances are that somewhere along the line some of them will have left behind wills, outlining what they wanted to happen to their possessions after their death.

Wills are a truly remarkable source for family historians: not only do they contain invaluable information about family relationships, but the fact that they were written by our ancestors themselves gives them the sort of authority and authenticity that documents created by the government or the Church so often lack.

A couple of crucial points to consider before you start a search for a will. First of all you should be aware that prior to the passing of the Married Women's Property Act in 1881 you will not, as a rule, find wills for married women, only for widows and spinsters. It's also important to remember that until fairly recent times the vast majority of the population, men or women, simply didn't leave a will. That's not to say that you shouldn't look for one, just that you shouldn't be too surprised if you don't find one.

It's time now to familiarize yourself with another important date on the family history calendar. On 12 January 1858, a new civic system of proving wills (i.e. the process by which a will was accepted as a legally valid document) was introduced. Since medieval times, the responsibility of proving wills had been in the hands of the Church of England through a vast network of ecclesiastical courts; now the state took over, and district probate registries were set up around the country to handle the process.

So, whenever you're planning a search for an ancestor's will, the first question to ask yourself is whether the person died before or after 1858, and your search will be very different depending on the answer.

Wills since 1858

Searching for a will that was proved on or after 12 January 1858 is a relatively straightforward process. Annual indexes (known as calendars) to all wills proved in England and Wales have been produced right from the start of the civil probate system. Your biggest problem here may be finding copies of the calendars, as they are not available on the internet, and paper and microfiche copies are rare.

A full set of calendars is held by the Principal Registry of the Family Division in their reading rooms at First Avenue House in London. Some of the district registries also have copies, although many have given their sets to their local county record office. A small number of sets of microfiche covering the years 1858 to 1943 have also been produced, and copies of these are available at the Family Records Centre and at The National Archives in Kew. The Society of Genealogists has a set of microfilm copies of the calendars from 1858 to 1930.

The entries in the calendars provide the family historian with some very useful information. A typical entry will tell you:

- the date of probate
- the deceased's full name
- their occupation
- when they died
- where they died
- where they lived
- where the will was proved
- the names, residences, occupations and relationships of two or more executors
- the value of the deceased's estate

Remember, all of this is just from the entry in the calendar. In fact, there isn't a great deal of information on a death certificate that you don't get here, and for this reason many people see little point in spending money on a certificate if they've found a corresponding entry in the will indexes. However, the deceased's age and the cause of death are crucial details which are not found in the calendars so, if you can, it's really best to get both. In 1892 the format of the calendars changed, and from this date there is significantly less detail in each entry.

Wills before 1858

Before 1858, the situation is much more complicated. There were more than a hundred church courts where wills could be proved; there is no centralized index and the surviving records of the courts are now spread around the country in local and county record offices. The system was based on the hierarchy of the ancient English ecclesiastical jurisdictions with the provinces of Canterbury and York at the top of the tree, a number of dioceses underneath (each made up of various archdeaconries and deaneries) and with the smaller 'peculiar' courts at the bottom. In practical terms this means that wherever your ancestors lived, their wills could have been proved in one of three or four different courts, and you will have to search the records of each of these in order to establish whether they left a will or not.

The surviving records are likely to include:

- the original wills submitted to the court
- a series of registered copies entered into ledgers by the court's clerks
- a set of contemporary manuscript indexes

Over the years, a number of record offices and local and family history societies have compiled and published various will indexes, and some record offices have produced card indexes to their own holdings. But by far the most significant change in more recent years has been the advent of online probate indexes, in some cases allowing access to digital images of the wills themselves.

The most important of these online resources (and by far the largest) is the National Archives' Documents Online website at *www.nationalarchives.gov.uk/documentsonline*.

The website provides full access to the entire collection of wills proved in the Prerogative Court of Canterbury – known more conveniently to family historians as the PCC. This was the senior court of probate for England and Wales, covering the whole of the province of Canterbury – basically the southern two-thirds of England and almost all of Wales.

The PCC also had responsibility for the wills of

English and Welsh citizens who died overseas or
in other parts of the United Kingdom. The collection of over one million wills dating from 1383 to
1858 includes some of the most famous names
in English history: William Shakespeare, Jane
Austen, Sir Isaac Newton, Lord Nelson, William
Wordsworth, to name but a few.

And while it's certainly true that the majority
of the wills proved in the PCC relate to people
from the upper echelons of society – the nobility
and gentry, military officers, merchants, lawyers,
clergyman and large landowners – the records
also include the wills of many small farmers, artisans, tradesmen, soldiers and sailors, and even
some agricultural labourers.

The Prerogative Court of York (the PCY) ful-
filled a similar role for England's northern counties. The records of the PCY are now held by the
Borthwick Institute in York.

As you move down the hierarchy of ecclesiastical probate courts you'll find increasingly large
numbers of wills of 'ordinary' people, and particularly back in the 17th century – in the period
before the Industrial Revolution – there's a good
chance that you might come across a will or two
in the family. If you do, you're in for yet another
family history treat.

Interpreting wills

There is simply no limit to the amount of useful detail you could find in a will. At the very least you are likely to get the testator's occupation and place of residence as well as the names of his wife and children, but you may also discover previously unknown nephews and nieces, uncles, aunts and cousins, and it's not uncommon for more distant relatives to be mentioned. You may also come across references to earlier generations if, for example, the testator refers to an item which was bequeathed to him by a parent or even a grandparent.

As well as providing you with all of this essential information, wills can give you a fascinating insight into your ancestors' lives, often listing personal possessions or tools connected with their trade. Just occasionally, you might come across evidence of a family quarrel where, for example, the eldest son was 'cut off with a shilling' or one of the children was left out of the will altogether, but you need to be careful about how you interpret the size of the bequests. The fact that one child was left significantly less than the others may be because they had already received a sum of money in their father's lifetime.

There are a number of problems that may confront you when you first come to read a will: there's the lack of regular punctuation, the use of archaic terms and the occasional Latin word here or there, but it's probably the unfamiliar handwriting that will cause you the greatest difficulty. The best advice is to get a photocopy of the will and take it home to read at your leisure. Don't try to work out every word first time through – if you get stuck on a particular word, carry on and come back to it later. The more you read old wills, the better you will get at recognizing the strange characters and styles that were used by the clerks – it really is a matter of experience.

Most wills before 1858 followed a fairly standard format. They usually started with the words '*In the name of God Amen*', reflecting both the ecclesiastical background to the process of proving wills and the highly religious nature of the society in which our ancestors lived their lives. Next came the testator's name, occupation and residence, followed by the date of the will and a statement that the testator was either '*in good and perfect health, mind and memory*' or possibly '*sick in body but whole in mind*' – the important point here was that he was fully rational and *compos mentis* at the time that the will was written. The testator often left detailed instructions

Did you know?
The year 1752 saw two major changes to the calendar. Until then, the year had always started on 25 March; now, as part of the adoption of the Gregorian calendar, New Year's Day would be 1 January. Additionally, and more controversially, 11 days were lost in September in order to bring England into line with the rest of Western Europe.

regarding his burial and then, with all these preliminaries out of the way, got on to the real business of the will – making sure that his nearest and dearest got their just deserts.

Working out exactly what the testator was trying to say can be a frustrating process – it's easy to lose track of where you are in a particular sentence as it rambles on into yet another sub-clause. It's clear that 17th-century solicitors weren't familiar with the idea of writing in Plain English! And as we move into the 1800s wills start to get longer and longer, with increasingly complicated bequests and more and more detailed instructions on how the deceased's estate should be disposed of.

It's a good idea to read through the will, make notes of the various bequests, the places and the personal names that are mentioned in it, and create your own summary. As well as being a useful exercise in itself, this will prove valuable as a quick reference point when planning future research or assessing what you know about the family.

Administrations and inventories

Before we leave the world of probate, there are a couple of other documents to look at that are closely associated with wills.

If a person died without leaving a will, letters of administration could be granted to their next of kin or another person who had a claim to the deceased's estate. Letters of administration (commonly known as admons) were granted by the same courts that were responsible for proving wills, with the same change in 1858 from an ecclesiastical to a civil system. In fact, the post-1858 national indexes to admons are combined with the probate calendars, which makes searching for these documents quite straightforward. Unfortunately for our purposes, the amount of information that you got on letters of administration is quite limited: usually just the name, date of death, residence and occupation of the deceased, as well as the name of the administrator together with their occupation, place of residence and relationship to the deceased. Occasionally, there may be some other detail which could provide you with vital information about the family, and it's always worth checking for an admon if your search for a will was unsuccessful. However, you certainly shouldn't assume that because there isn't a will there must be an admon – this is far from being the case.

It was not uncommon before the late 1700s for an inventory to be taken, listing the deceased's personal possessions, often on a room-by-room basis, together with the value of each item and a total value of the estate. And if you're fortunate enough to come across an inventory for a member of your family you should get a fascinating insight into their daily life. Inventories don't survive in huge numbers but, again, it's always worth checking to see if there's one to accompany an ancestor's will.

Death duty records

Both admons and inventories are usually kept together with the collections of wills among the records of the old ecclesiastical courts, but there's another source, closely related to wills, for which we have to thank the Inland Revenue. A vast series of registers was kept between the years 1796 and 1903 recording the payments of a series of taxes known collectively as death duty. Copies of all wills proved in England and Wales were sent by the various probate courts to the Inland Revenue, where clerks began their work by abstracting the details of the various bequests and beneficiaries and copying the information into their registers.

The death duty registers have a particular value for family historians for a number of reasons. First of all, they identify the name of the court where the will was proved, which in the absence of a pre-1858 national probate index can save you a great deal of searching. Second, the registers were living, working documents: the Inland Revenue went to great pains to ensure that they collected every penny due to them, and information about the payments of the duty was recorded meticulously and in great detail. Therefore, if they learnt that a beneficiary had died, the date of death would be noted; if an executor moved house, the new address was entered; if a daughter married, her married name was recorded. Sometimes a will might simply indicate that the testator had a number of children, while the equivalent entry in the death duty registers might actually name them. You could even learn about children who were born after the testator wrote his will.

There are, admittedly, a few difficulties that

you might encounter with using the registers. For a start, you'll need to be able to get to the National Archives in Kew or the Family Records Centre in London to view the documents (the FRC only has copies of the registers up to 1858). Second, when you do get to see the registers, you'll find that they can be quite difficult to interpret, to say the least. Their very nature, as working documents, can lead to problems. The notes made by the Inland Revenue's clerks, recording the receipt of new information concerning the case, are often written in a heavily abbreviated style which can sometimes obscure their meaning. The clerks clearly knew what they meant at the time but it's not always obvious to us today, and after several years of annotations an entry in the registers can become quite confusing. The entries were only 'closed' once the Inland Revenue were satisfied either that they had collected all the tax due, or that the estate was for one reason or another exempt from payment of duty. And since examples have been found of notes being entered in the registers more than seventy years after a file was opened, you can imagine just how congested the entries can become.

All of these records can be extremely useful in your research, both for the vast amount of information they can provide you with and for the number of other records that they can lead you into. The most obvious are records of deaths and burials, but they can also suggest links to census returns, births and baptisms, marriages and even more 'advanced' sources concerning land ownership and legal disputes. Wills are a vital resource for family historians, and although accessing and interpreting the records may present you with some difficulties, you should make every possible effort to track them down and take the time to learn what they're telling us about the lives of our ancestors.

Wills and probate: some useful terms

Administrator A person who is appointed to administer the estate of an *intestate* or to administer in default of an executor named in a will. A woman appointed in this way is known as an *administratrix*.

Annuity An income or allowance received annually.

Appurtenances Something that belongs to something else. For example, the land in which a house is situated.

Assign or assignee A person who is appointed to act in place of another, often found in the phrase '*heirs and assigns*'.

Beneficiary A person who is left something in a will.

Codicil A supplement to a will.

Executor A person appointed by the testator to ensure that his wishes are carried out. A female appointed in this way is known as an *executrix*.

Heir The person who is legally entitled to succeed to another's property.

Hereditaments Property that can be inherited.

Imprimis First (Latin).

Intestate A person who dies without leaving a will.

Messuage A house or dwelling-place together with its appurtenances.

Personal estate A person's moveable property not including land and buildings, etc.

Probate Proving a will. The act of making it a legally binding document.

Real estate The land and buildings, etc. (i.e. not moveable property) owned by a person.

Testator A man who makes a will. A woman is known as a *testatrix*.

Check it out

As we have already seen, the documents we use for
our family history research were not designed with us
in mind, nor are they necessarily arranged in a way
that makes it easy for us to find the information
we're looking for. In order to address this problem
there has been a huge effort over the years on the
part of record offices and archives, commercial
organizations, record societies, family and local history groups and hundreds of dedicated individuals to
make the records we use more accessible.

Thousands of indexes to large collections of documents have been produced, listing the names and
other important details of the people they relate to.
Recently this effort has been concentrated on producing electronic resources either on CD or on the
internet. The work of indexing the records that we
use today began in earnest back in the 19th century,
when enthusiastic antiquarians started to recognize
the importance of Britain's vast wealth of historical
records and set about the task of preserving them
for posterity. Documents like parish registers, poll
books, tax returns and medieval legal records were
among the most popular records for the antiquarians to tackle.

Since the 1970s the focus has very much moved
to indexing census returns and wills, and family

history societies have been particularly active in producing census indexes for their own areas of interest. Using a vast army of volunteers, almost 80 per cent of the returns for 1851 have been indexed and big sections of the other years have been covered.

In the mid 1980s a project to index the 1881 census returns for the whole of England, Wales and Scotland began, and despite taking over ten years to complete, it showed the family history world that such a mammoth task was possible and helped to establish certain standards and principles for future indexing projects. This venture – a joint effort involving the Church of Jesus Christ of Latter-day Saints (the Mormons), the Federation of Family History Societies and the Public Record Office – was an excellent example of how different organizations could work together to a common end.

The Mormons are also behind what is certainly the single most significant index for family historians. The International Genealogical Index (commonly known as the IGI) brings together several hundred million records of births and marriages either extracted from parish registers or submitted by members of the Church of Jesus Christ of Latter-day Saints. Every serious family historian will at some time in the course of their research have cause to consult the IGI – it is quite simply indispensable.

However, the crucial point to bear in mind about

all of these indexes is that they are a means of accessing the documents and not a replacement for them. However good it is, however comprehensive and accurate it may be, using an index is simply no substitute for viewing the original document itself.

Never rely on what you find in an index – instead, use the information you get as a way into the documents. For a start, the index may contain errors — after all, the person who transcribed the details from the original may not have been entirely familiar with the handwriting or with the names of the people or places. But, more importantly, the original may contain additional information — information which may give you vital clues about your family.

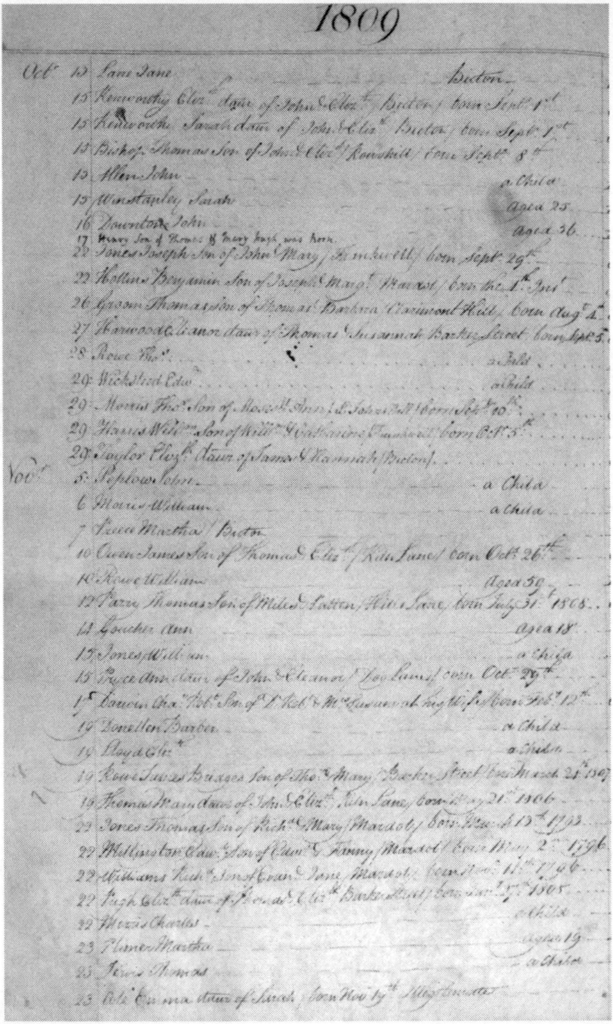

Page from the parish register of St Chad's, Shrewsbury, showing the baptism of Charles Darwin, 1809.

Chapter 7

Parcels of the past: records before 1837

- A brief history of parish registers
- Latin in parish registers
  Important Latin words in family history records
- Later parish registers
- Dade registers
- Before you start
- The International Genealogical Index
- Other parish register indexes
- Marriage indexes for family historians
- Searching in parish registers

If you have a successful passage through the records we've looked at in the previous chapters, you will eventually reach the point where you're searching for an ancestor who was born prior to the start of civil registration in 1837. And provided that you've done your research thoroughly and you've used the records to their full potential, you should by now have enough information on your ancestor to fully arm yourself for the big adventure that's about to begin.

A brief history of parish registers

In 1538, King Henry VIII ordered that registers should be kept recording all the baptisms, marriages and burials that took place in each parish. There were some early teething problems – many parsons, vicars and curates were unsure about exactly what information was to be recorded, and although the entries were supposed to be made in a register book, many ended up on loose sheets of paper. In 1598 a further order was approved by Queen Elizabeth in an attempt to tighten up the system. Parchment registers were to be purchased by every parish and duplicate copies were to be sent to the relevant bishop's court. At the same time the names from the earlier registers were supposed to be copied into these new bound registers. However, many clerks ignored the first 20 years and started in 1558 (the first year of Queen Elizabeth's reign) and fewer than 800 registers are known to start as early as 1538. Only a handful of Welsh parish registers commence in the 16th century.

The duplicate copies of the registers (known as bishops' transcripts) have survived in large numbers to the present day and are usually held by diocesan record offices – which in most cases are also the county record offices. As well as being an important alternative source for family historians, these transcripts are a useful measure against fraud – after all, there's very little point in altering an entry in the local parish register if the bishop has his own copy securely stored away.

Most of the earliest surviving registers are composite registers, covering baptisms, marriages and burials in a single volume, and the entries in them are somewhat lacking in detail. Each entry consists of the date of the event followed by the most basic information: the baptisms rarely recorded more than the name of the child and the father's name, the marriages would usually give the names of both parties but are unlikely to tell you anything else about them, while the burial entries often consisted of nothing more than the name of the deceased.

Latin in parish registers

Some of these early registers were written in Latin, but this shouldn't present too big a problem as most of the entries are in a fairly standard format.

Important Latin words in family history records

son	*filius*
daughter	*filia*
wife	*uxor*
father	*pater*
mother	*mater*
baptized	*baptisatus*
married	*in matrimonium ducere*
buried	*sepultus*
age in years	*aetatis*
widow	*vidue*
deceased	*defuncti*

Remember that Latin words have different endings depending on the context and on whether the subject is male or female – for example, the Latin for buried is *sepultus* but if the person being buried was female, the word used would be *sepulta*. Even personal names can have different endings – the name Robert in Latin is *Robertus* but 'Robert, son of Robert' would be

Robertus filius Roberti. There are many useful books and websites which cover this subject in much greater depth.

Later parish registers

Gradually, the amount of detail in the registers increased: it began to be normal to show the mother's name on baptisms, marriages would show the bride or groom's parish if they were marrying away from home, and burial entries recording the age of the deceased started to become more common.

During the 17th and early 18th centuries, increasingly large numbers of people began to marry outside the established Church of England. By the late 1740s the government had become seriously concerned about the problem of so-called clandestine or irregular marriages, which, although perfectly legal, were usually conducted by disreputable clergymen and were open to all sorts of abuse and fraud. Most took place in one of a number of notorious venues in London such as the precincts of the Fleet Prison, the Mayfair Chapel and Holy Trinity Minories, and since there was little or no control over them bigamous marriages were quite common.

In order to deal with this growing problem,

Hardwicke's Marriage Act was passed by Parliament. By the terms of this Act, which came into force in 1754, it became illegal to marry outside the Church of England. From now on all marriages had to be performed in one of two ways – either after banns or by licence. And they had to be recorded in a dedicated marriage register with individually numbered pages and entries – a means of ensuring that the details were properly recorded and an effective safeguard against fraud.

So from 1754 until the start of civil registration in 1837, unless your ancestors were Jewish or Quakers (both were specifically exempted from Hardwicke's Act), you should expect to find their marriages recorded in the Church of England's parish registers.

The registers showed the names of the bride and groom as well as their parish of residence and their marital status. If either of them was a minor (i.e. aged under 21) this will be recorded, and the register will always show whether the marriage was by licence or banns. You will also find the signatures (or marks) of both parties, together with the signatures of two or more witnesses – and remember that the signatures you see here are the ones that were actually written by your ancestors, which might be as much as two hundred years ago.

In 1813, pre-printed registers were introduced for baptisms and burials, and from this date the entries in most parish registers are of a standard format. The baptismal registers recorded the following details:

- when baptized
- child's Christian name
- parents' name:
  - Christian
  - surname
- abode
- quality, trade or profession
- by whom the ceremony was performed

Much of this information is the same as you would expect to find on the post-1837 civil registration birth certificates – the only two details which are lacking here are the date of birth and the mother's maiden name.

In fact, the date of birth *is* quite often given, particularly in cases of multiple baptisms where two or more children from the same family were baptized at the same time. And although most children were baptized when they were only a month or two old, it's important to bear in mind that the baptism could take place several months or even years later.

The pre-printed burial registers from 1813

onwards provided the following information:
- name
- abode
- when buried
- age
- by whom the ceremony was performed

As you can see, the amount of information here is fairly limited. There's no space for the deceased's occupation, which was sometimes given in burial registers before 1813, and, more importantly, there's nothing whatsoever about the deceased's relationship to anyone else. But in most cases there should be enough to enable you to identify your ancestors.

The middle of the 19th century saw the advent of municipal cemeteries, and in most urban areas you shouldn't expect to find too many church burials after about 1855. Some cemetery registers have been deposited with county record offices but most are still in the care of the cemeteries themselves, while many are held by the relevant local authorities.

The pre-printed registers which were introduced in 1813 are still in use today, and although after 1837 they are perhaps not considered a major source for family historians, they certainly shouldn't be ignored. Parish registers do have

Dade registers

If you're very lucky you may find that your ancestors came from a parish where a special type of register known as a Dade register was in use. Named after the Reverend William Dade, the man who was primarily responsible for their introduction, the registers are a gold mine. They normally record not only the child's name and parents' names, but also give details of both sets of grandparents and often give additional information about the parents, like *their* places of birth. Dade burial registers normally give the deceased's father's name, and you may even find the cause of death given. Unfortunately, these registers are mostly from parishes in Yorkshire but there are also a few from Lancashire, Nottinghamshire and Cheshire and similar registers are occasionally found in parts of Wiltshire, Somerset and Berkshire.

certain advantages over the equivalent civil registration records. For a start, the registers are held locally (normally in the appropriate county record office) where access to them is both straightforward and free. Second, because you can search at your leisure through the registers of a particular parish, it's fairly easy to pick out not just your direct ancestors but also their siblings, cousins and in-laws.

Before you start

There are a few questions that you'll need to ask yourself before you start searching for your ancestors in parish registers. For example, if you're looking for a baptism, do you have all the information you need to carry out an effective search? Do you know:

- approximately when they were born?
- where they were born?
- their father's name?

If the person you're looking for was born in the first few decades of the 19th century then you'll probably have all this from the research you've done previously – you should have their age and place of birth from the censuses and their father's name from their marriage certificate. But once you start working further back in time you'll soon find that identifying the correct entry becomes increasingly difficult.

And the biggest problem you'll come up against is knowing *where* to search for your ancestors, because they had this annoying habit of moving around from village to village and once you get back into the 18th century you won't have census returns to help you track their movements. But now for the good news: for over a hundred years the Church of Jesus Christ of Latter-day Saints (the Mormons) have been extracting information from parish registers, and the result of their labour is now available as part of the world's biggest family history database – the International Genealogical Index.

The International Genealogical Index

The IGI contains several hundred million entries mainly relating to the births, baptisms and marriages of people who lived between about 1500 and 1880; it doesn't as a rule contain information about living people, and you won't find records of deaths or burials.

The index is made up of two very different types of records; the majority are the results of a worldwide 'extraction programme', but there are also vast numbers of 'patron submissions'. The extractions are of far more significance to us as family historians since they represent the nearest thing we have to a centralized index to parish registers. The patron submissions are records of research by individual members of the Church of Latter-day Saints, and while much of the research may well be sound, there is no quality control in place and you really should treat the submitted entries with extreme caution. If you come across the record of a John Smith, born around 1700 in London, you might want to ask yourself whether this is the result of reliable research or an example of pure guesswork. Whether you're looking at the IGI online, on CD-ROM or on microfiche, you should always check the source of the information, and if you see the words 'Record submitted by a member of the LDS Church' you should think twice before accepting the entry at face value.

And while the IGI is without doubt the most indispensable of resources for family historians all around the world, you should always bear in mind that it is by no means a comprehensive record of all baptisms and marriages. Its coverage is patchy, to say the least: some parts of the country are well served (Cornwall, Durham, Lincolnshire and Shropshire, for example) while others (such as Dorset, Norfolk and Wiltshire) have relatively few entries. You should never assume that the absence of an entry for your ancestor means that she wasn't baptized. If the parish where she was born isn't covered by the IGI then you wouldn't expect to find a record of her baptism there. And if you find an entry which looks quite promising but doesn't quite fit, try to resist the temptation to accept the entry as yours, and consider the possibility that your ancestor might simply have been baptized in a neighbouring parish which isn't covered by the IGI.

Having said all this, the IGI should always be your first port of call once you arrive in the pre-civil registration era.

When you find an entry which appears to relate to your ancestor, the first thing you need to do is to ask yourself whether you can prove 'beyond reasonable doubt' that the entry you've found is the right one. If the name you're looking for is relatively uncommon, or if you're working with a very distinctive middle name, your search will be that much easier. But you need to consider all the issues regarding names that we looked at in the earlier chapter on births, and it's particularly important to remember that the further back you go the more you need to be on the lookout for alternative spellings of names – first names as well as surnames.

The IGI is particularly useful on this last point as it groups similar names together. So whether your ancestor is recorded as Robert or Robt. a search should find him. It also includes Latin forms of names, so Robertus would show up too. Surnames work in the same way: a search for the name HIBBERT would bring up alternative spellings such as HIBBARD, HIBBART and HEB-BARD as well as less obvious variants like IBBETT, IBBOTS and HIBARTE. You do have the option to search for exact spellings of names but in most cases this is not advisable.

Other parish register indexes

The IGI isn't the only index that you can use to help you with your parish register searches. The British Isles Vital Records Index is another useful resource produced by the Mormons. It's very similar in format and content to the IGI, and although it is a much smaller database the second edition contains over 12 million births, baptisms and marriages (again, no deaths or burials). And all of these entries are extractions from original sources rather than submissions.

There are also two dedicated marriage indexes which you will almost certainly find helpful in your research. Pallot's Marriage Index was started by a firm of record agents in 1813 and contains 1.5 million marriages, and although it's particularly strong for London and Middlesex it also has many thousands of entries from other parts of the country. The index covers the years 1780 to

1837 and is practically complete in this period for the city of London.

Family historians have many reasons to be grateful to the late Percival Boyd. Boyd began his greatest project in 1925 and the result is an index to more than six million marriage entries taken from parish registers the length and breadth of the country. It covers the years 1538 to 1837 and has excellent coverage for certain counties, such as Cambridgeshire, Essex and Suffolk, although in some cases there are few entries after 1753.

There are also hundreds of smaller marriage indexes compiled by family history societies, local record offices or enterprising individuals. The best guide to accessing these indexes is the Gibson and Hampson guide *Marriage and Census Indexes for Family Historians* (*see* Further reading).

Remember: the International Genealogical Index, the British Isles Vital Records Index, Pallot's and Boyd's are indexes, not primary sources – you should always check the original parish register entry.

Very few parish registers (other than the ones that are still in use) are held in parish churches. The vast majority have been deposited in the relevant county record office although some are held in local studies libraries. There are a number

Marriage indexes for family historians

Index name	Coverage	Medium
The International Genealogical Index	Worldwide	Online (FamilySearch) CD-ROM Microfiche
British Isles Vital Records Index	England, Wales Scotland and Ireland	CD-ROM
Pallot's Marriage Index	England and Wales (but mainly London)	Online (Ancestry.com) CD-ROM Paper slips (IHGS, Canterbury)
Boyd's Marriage Index	England and Wales	Online (British Origins.com) Microfiche Typescript volumes (Society of Genealogists)

of excellent resources which will tell you where the original registers are held, and the best is *The Phillimore Atlas & Index of Parish Registers*.

Now in its third edition, this essential tome is known to many as the bible of family historians. The atlas is divided into two sections; the first includes a series of maps (one for each English county, three covering Wales) showing the location of each ancient parish together with the starting dates of the earliest surviving parish registers. For each county there is also a separate topographical map dating from 1834 showing the main roads and other features, which should help you to place your ancestor's village or town in its local context.

The second section consists of a series of county lists that record a remarkable amount of information for each parish, including the earliest and latest dates of its deposited registers; the coverage on the IGI and various other marriage indexes; and the name of the relevant civil registration district. These lists also act as an index to the maps and, most important of all, they indicate where the original parish registers are now held. The latest edition of *The Phillimore Atlas & Index of Parish Registers* also includes a similar series of parish maps and county lists for Scotland.

Another excellent source is the multi-volume *National Index of Parish Registers*, which lists, county by county, all the known surviving parish registers together with their covering dates, information about indexes, copies and transcripts and the whereabouts of the originals.

Many county record offices have put lists of their parish register holdings online, and their websites may be more up to date than the printed sources, listing newly deposited registers and other recent acquisitions. Many local studies centres and larger libraries also hold copies of the parish registers for their own areas, and the Society of Genealogists has a huge collection of microfilms and transcripts of literally thousands of parish registers. The Society's website has a list of their parish register holdings: consult at *www.sog.org.uk/prc/index.html.* The website is regularly updated.

As well as indexing millions of records from parish registers, the Church of Jesus Christ of Latter-day Saints has also undertaken a huge microfilming programme, and you can access copies of thousands of English and Welsh parish registers through their family history centres. You'll probably have to pay a small fee and wait a week or two for the microfilm to arrive, but if your ancestors lived hundreds of miles away, and you can't easily get to the relevant county record office, this may be a cheaper and also a more convenient option for you.

Searching in parish registers

If the registers you need to search haven't been indexed then you'll have to grit your teeth and prepare for what could be a long and challenging search. The post-1812 registers are fairly easy to search (although in the bigger urban parishes, finding as many as fifty baptisms being per-formed each week is not at all uncommon, so you may still be in for a lengthy search) but the earlier registers can be quite troublesome. The general standard of handwriting leaves a lot to be desired, and in many cases you'll find baptisms and burials and sometimes even marriages mixed in together on the same page. The best approach is not to rush your search – it's so easy to miss a vital entry if you're not concentrating properly or if you're scanning a page too quickly.

It's a good idea, particularly if you're searching in a rural area, to make a note of any other entries you happen upon with the surname that you're looking for. If it's a common name you may find too many entries, most of which have no connection whatsoever to your family, but if you're dealing with a fairly uncommon name any instance of it in your ancestor's parish is worth noting, as it may turn out to be a relative. You should certainly note down any siblings of your direct ancestors that you come across – it all helps to build up the picture of your ancestors' lives in the parish and, of course, the baptism of the first child will help you in your search for the parents' marriage.

An important point to bear in mind when searching for a marriage (if you haven't been able to find it in one of the various indexes we've looked at) is that the couple normally married in the bride's parish. Until fairly recent times, only a small minority of people moved more than about twenty miles from their place of birth during the course of their lives. They may have moved frequently from one village to another seeking work, but they tended to stay within their own 'country', an area centred on a market town which served as both a trading post and a meeting place. The regular markets with their gatherings of farmers, tradesmen and labourers provided a great opportunity for people from different villages to meet and get to know each other. This would have been the way that many of our ancestors met their future husbands and wives, and it helps to explain why men so often ended up marrying women from relatively distant parishes. It was also fairly common for women to return to their home parish for their first confinement, so you may find that the oldest child was baptized in a different parish from the rest.

By far the biggest problem with searching in parish registers is that there is absolutely nothing in them which explicitly links one record to another. A baptism will show the names of the child's parents but not its mother's maiden name, so identifying a corresponding marriage may be a difficult task. And while it may be obvious that the marriage of John WILKINSON and Mary BROWN that you found in 1785 ties in with the baptisms of those children of John and Mary WILKINSON in the same parish starting in 1786, if the children had all been born in different parishes you might have had some difficulty tracking them down. And if you were coming at the problem from the opposite direction, and had found the baptisms of these children, proving that they all belonged to the same family would be far from straightforward.

There are a number of techniques you can use to help overcome these problems. The most useful is a method known as family reconstitution, which involves extracting all the references to a particular surname from the registers of a specific parish or a number of neighbouring

Did you know?
The phrase 'of full age' which is frequently found on marriage certificates in the early years of civil registration means that the person in question was aged 21 years or more.

parishes over a number of years and using the information to build up likely family groups. This research can then be backed up with information from other sources such as wills, manorial documents and legal records. It's not a foolproof process and it can be very time consuming, but it's often the only approach that will produce results.

In the three hundred years before the start of civil registration, parish registers represent the single most important source for family historians. There were over 12,000 ancient parishes in England and Wales, and the registers kept by those parishes are a vast and unique collection, recording the lives of many millions of English and Welsh men and women over nearly five hundred years of our history. The fact that they have survived the ravages of time is testament to the relative stability that the country has known over this period. With the notable exception of the English Civil War in the middle of the 17th century, there have been no major interruptions to the process of recording the vital events in our ancestors' lives.

When the system of registers was first set up in 1538 the intention was to record every baptism, marriage and burial taking place within each parish; however, the rise of English Protestant nonconformity meant that the registers ceased to be a complete record of these events as more and more people moved to new places of worship, and away from the established Church of England.

Family, friends and neighbours

There are two main ways of drawing up a family tree: you can either start from yourself and work upwards, or start with your oldest known ancestor and work down through the generations. Neither method is intrinsically 'better' than the other, but there's a real danger that if you only use the bottom-up (pedigree) method to record the results of your research you're not really looking at the whole picture. Pedigrees only show your direct ancestors – your parents, grand-parents, great grandparents, and so on. Brothers and sisters, nephews and nieces, aunts, uncles and cousins are nowhere to be seen, and yet if you're not fully investigating them and their lives it's not really a *family* history at all.

Finding out about these relatives, getting to know more about your ancestors' extended families, is a great way to increase your knowledge of the family as a whole and to help you get a better understanding of what your ancestors' lives were really like. And if you're only looking at your direct ancestors you may miss some vital clues.

You should really aim to track down all of your ancestors' siblings in each of the census returns. Information about their ages, places of birth and occupations can point you in unexpected directions or suggest new areas of interesting research. An uncle's will might mention your direct ancestor – as a beneficiary or even an executor – and your great great grandfather might have been a witness at the wedding of one of his brothers or sisters.

So while you may concentrate the main efforts of your research on your direct lines, you should never ignore the other family members and the additional information that the records of their lives can add to the story of your family.

And you shouldn't ignore your ancestors' neighbours, either. The people that your family rubbed shoulders with, day in, day out, almost certainly had a significant impact on their lives. When you find your ancestors in the census returns, you should make a point of looking at the other families living nearby. The occupations will give you an idea of the sort of area they lived in – and it's possible that the neighbours were also relatives, not just in rural areas. Even in large towns and cities it wasn't at all uncommon to find siblings, cousins or in-laws living next door.

Family history is not about individuals: it's about families and the communities that they lived in. And if you always try to extend your research beyond the immediate family you should be richly rewarded.

Catherine Emily, Daughter of Robert

119 Waring Darwin M. D and Susanna his
wife of the Parish of St Chad Shrewsbury
the County of Salop (born May the 9th 1810)
was baptized May 19th 1810 by one George Case

Protestant Dissenting Minister

120 George Henry son of George Case & Esther his wife
of the parish of St Chad Shrewsbury in the county
of Salop born the 9th of august 1810, was baptized
by me the 23d of october 1810,   W. Hazlitt

Protestant Dissenting Minister
of Wem

George Son of Robt Davies and Elizabeth his wife
121 of the Parish of St Mary Shrewsbury in the County
of Salop (born the 28th of November 1811) was
baptized Dec'r the 29th 1811, by me George Case

Protestant Dissenting Minister

John Mettimore Son of William Healing and
122 Ann his Wife of the Parish of St Chad Shrewsbury
in the County of Salop (born Nov'r 26th 1811) was baptized
Jan'y 7th 1812 — by me George Case

Protestant Dissenting Minister

123 Bithia Daughter of Thomas Small and Margaret his
wife of the Parish of St Mary Shrewsbury in the County
of Salop (born January the 7th 1813) was baptized
April the 8th 1813 by me George Case

Protestant Dissenting Minister

Page from the Presbyterian Chapel register, Shrewsbury, showing the
baptism of Catherine Emily Darwin (Charles Darwin's sister), 1810.

Chapter 8

Other directions: more record sources

- Nonconformist registers
- Other associated registers
- Dr Williams's Library
- The Wesleyan Methodist Metropolitan Registry
- The Fleet Marriage Registers
- Roman Catholic records
- Jewish records

The history of English nonconformity can be traced back as far as the 14th century. But it wasn't until the second half of the 17th century that groups of likeminded 'dissenters' started to become organized and to develop their own identities.

The term 'nonconformist' is used to describe any Protestant who does not conform to the doctrines and usages of the established Church of England. By the start of the 19th century, nonconformists made up around a quarter of the population of England and Wales. And this figure has a significant impact on our family history research, since it would suggest that the baptisms of as many as a quarter of our ancestors won't be recorded in the Church of England's parish registers.

Over the years a number of distinct groups emerged: Quakers, Baptists, Independents (also known as Congregationalists), Presbyterians, Methodists, Unitarians and many more. Each had their own individual beliefs (mostly to do with how the church should be run rather than any major doctrinal differences) and the boundaries between the various denominations were often quite blurred; groups merged with each other or split off to form new sects. Some of the groups had hundreds of places of worship around the country, with huge numbers of people attending their weekly services, while other smaller denominations such as the Swedenborgians, the Inghamites and the Moravians consisted of just a few congregations.

Swelling the ranks of these groups were large numbers of Protestant immigrants who settled in England from the 16th century onwards. The most significant of these were the Huguenots: French Calvinists who fled to England to escape persecution in their own country. The Huguenots settled mainly in the East End of London, but there were also significant communities in several other towns and cities in the south and east of England, most notably Norwich, Plymouth and Canterbury. Calvinist exiles from the Netherlands also founded their own congregations in the south of England in the late 16th century.

Nonconformist registers

In 1837, as part of the establishment of the civil registration system, a registration commission was set up and the surviving registers of all these nonconformist congregations were called in by the newly formed General Register Office. Not all of the congregations complied with the request to surrender their registers (and it wasn't compulsory) but most did; and eventually, following a further call in 1858, over 6,000 registers were collected. The entire collection was later transferred to the Public Record Office (now The National Archives).

Very few of these registers date from before the Civil War period and it's unlikely that any of the English nonconformist congregations kept registers before then. The earliest registers in the National Archives' collection are those of the Protestant immigrant communities; the oldest, dating from 1567, is from the Southampton 'Walloon' church. The register of Hindley Presbyterian Church, Lancashire, is the earliest surviving English Protestant nonconformist register, with entries dating from 1642.

The standard of record-keeping differed greatly from one denomination to another. By far the best in terms of detail, accuracy and completeness are those of the Religious Society of Friends or, as they are more commonly known, the Quakers. The National Archives has copies of around 1,500 registers of births, deaths, burials and marriages of Quaker congregations from every corner of England and Wales. This is the largest collection of any single denomination, and when the records were catalogued by the Public Record Office they were placed in a series of their own.

Did you know?

Family history research is an important part of the doctrine of the Church of Jesus Christ of Latter-day Saints – the Mormon church. The Mormons have devoted considerable resources to gathering records, producing invaluable tools for the family historian: notably the International Genealogical Index (IGI). Church members use these resources to make 'covenants' on behalf of their deceased ancestors.

The registers of the Moravian Church represent another good example of meticulous record-keeping, and in addition to the usual records of baptisms, marriages and burials many of them contain a wealth of information about the history and administration of the congregation. This is a feature of many nonconformist registers: lists of ministers and members of the congregations, plans of churches and burial grounds, financial transactions, trust deeds, even transcripts of wills – all of these and more can be found in these registers. If you find a record of your ancestor in a nonconformist register, don't just note the details of their baptism and move on to the next task on your list – it's always worth having a look at the rest of the register to see if any extra information is included.

From 1754, the registers will, as a rule, contain

records of baptisms and burials only – under the terms of Hardwicke's Marriage Act, nonconformists were forced to marry within the established Church of England. However, Quakers were specifically exempted from this Act and the records of Quaker marriages are among the most extraordinary documents that you'll come across. As well as details of the bride and groom and the names and occupations of their parents, Quaker marriage certificates often include the names of as many as 50 witnesses, many of whom were probably relatives of the couple.

Since relatively few of the congregations had their own burial grounds, many nonconformists were buried in the Anglican parish churchyard, but most chose to have their children baptized in their own churches and chapels.

Nonconformist registers are generally more informative than their Anglican counterparts – the baptismal registers often recorded the mother's maiden name – but the amount of information included differs so much from one denomination to another, and even among different congregations of the same denomination, that it's probably best just to say that you'll find out when you get there!

Most of the registers held by the National Archives end in 1837, although there was also a second commission of 1858 which resulted in the deposit of another five hundred or so registers which are now held by the National Archives. And don't forget that the congregations continued to keep records of baptisms, burials and marriages (which could again take place in nonconformist chapels from 1 July 1837) beyond this date. Many of these later registers have been deposited in local or county record offices but some are still in the care of the congregations.

And now for some more good news: the International Genealogical Index (IGI) covers almost all of the baptisms recorded in the National Archives' collection of nonconformist registers (not the Quaker registers, though) so if you find a reference in the IGI to an event which appears to have taken place in a non-Anglican church it probably relates to one of these registers. And once you know that your ancestors were nonconformists and you know which denomination they belonged to, you can check the relevant burial registers for records of other family members.

Other associated registers

As well as the records of the many individual nonconformist congregations there are also several collections of registers of large multi-denominational burial grounds, such as Bunhill Fields, the Victoria Park Cemetery, Gibraltar Row, Golden Lane Cemetery and Southwark New Burial Ground in London, and the wonderfully named Necropolis Burial Ground in Liverpool.

Along with all these nonconformist registers, the General Register Office collected a number of registers that belonged to the Anglican Church but which were outside the normal parochial system. These include the registers of the British Lying-in Hospital in Holborn, the Greenwich and Chelsea Hospitals (for the Royal Navy and Army respectively) and other smaller institutions such as Mercers' Hall in Cheapside, London, and the Chapels Royal at Whitehall and Windsor.

Before we leave the subject of nonconformists and the records that they left behind, there are some other significant collections of records to consider.

Dr Williams's Library

Two Acts of Parliament were passed in the late 17th century which effectively prevented Protestant nonconformists and Roman Catholics from holding official positions in England and Wales. The Test and Corporation Acts meant that only people who had been baptized in the Anglican Church could sit on town councils, or hold commissions in the Army and Royal Navy, or teach at and even attend universities. In 1727 the General Body of Ministers of the Three Denominations was established to represent the views of the Presbyterians, Baptists and Independents (or Congregationalists) in the campaign for the repeal of the Test and Corporation Acts. The campaign was eventually successful, although it wasn't until 1828 that the Acts were overturned and nonconformists gained full religious freedom.

One of the many grievances that nonconformists held was that their baptismal registers had no legal standing and were not recognized by courts of law in matters of inheritance or intestacy. In 1742, as a small but significant part of their long campaign for religious equality, the Three Denominations started their own registry of births. The idea was to demonstrate that they could record birth details, issue certificates and produce accurate copies of these certificates – all in a highly efficient way and with an exceptional standard of record-keeping.

Initially, very few births were registered – only 309 are recorded in the first 26 years of the registry – but by the time the registry was closed in

December 1837 it included the details of almost 50,000 births. The registry was officially called the General Register of Protestant Dissenters, but over the years it has come to be known in the family history world as 'Dr Williams's Library' – named after the building in which it was housed from 1742 until 1837. It's an unfortunately misleading name, as not only does it not describe what the registry actually was, but it causes all sorts of problems for the staff of Dr Williams's Library, which is still in existence today. The registers are no longer held by the Library but were deposited with the General Register Office in the late 1830s and are now held by the National Archives.

The registry produced three different sets of documents: the original birth registers, a complete collection of the certificates issued by the registry and a set of contemporary indexes.

Finding records in the registers is not exactly straightforward. Although the indexes are accurate enough, they're not in strict alphabetical order; instead, the entries are listed chronologically by the initial letter of the surname. And the other factor which causes problems (although it's actually one of the reasons that the records are so useful for family historians) is that retrospective registration was actively encouraged. The registry was opened in 1742 but the earliest birth recorded dates from 1716 and several registrations have been found of people aged 50 or more. And it's important to bear in mind that the entry for a birth which took place in 1810 but wasn't registered until 1820 would appear in the index covering the later period, and of course you will have no way of knowing when or even if a particular birth was registered until you start searching.

Once more the Latter-day Saints have come to our rescue. Some 85 per cent of the entries in the Dr Williams's Library registers are indexed by the second edition of the British Isles Vital Records Index (BIVRI). Hopefully, the remaining entries will appear in the next edition, but even now the BIVRI is an excellent first port of call for a search in these remarkable registers.

And if you're lucky enough to have ancestors whose births were registered at Dr Williams's Library you really are in for a treat. In addition to the usual information that you might expect to find with a birth or baptism – the child's name, place and date of birth and the parents' names – you will usually get not just the mother's maiden name but also the names of *her* parents. All of this information should be fully recorded both on the copy certificates *and* in the registers, but it's always worth checking both sources as you may find that one contains more information than the other.

The Wesleyan Methodist Metropolitan Registry

In 1818, the Wesleyan Methodists started a very similar registry known as the Wesleyan Methodist Metropolitan Registry. The methods of record-keeping and the types of records used were essentially identical to those used by the Three Denominations in their registry, and although the Methodists' birth registry is somewhat smaller it does contain over 10,000 records, so it still represents a significant collection. The registry was officially closed in December 1837 but the final entry in the records was made on 7 January 1840.

The British Isles Vital Records Index covers most of the records in this registry but there is also a contemporary index which you can use as a backup.

Many of the births included in the Wesleyan Methodists' registry may also be recorded in one of the many Methodist baptismal registers held by the National Archives, and you should be able to access these through the International Genealogical Index.

The Fleet Marriage Registers

This is one of the most curious collections of registers held by the National Archives and they have a strange and chequered history. The registers were originally kept by the clergymen who performed the marriage ceremonies and were in effect their personal property. When Hardwicke's Marriage Act became law in 1754 the various marriage chapels were closed down, and at this stage many of the registers are thought to have been destroyed or simply lost.

However, a few enterprising individuals began to gather together the surviving registers and in 1821 they were purchased by the government. They eventually ended up in the Public Record Office and were grouped together with the larger collections of nonconformist registers. But they are in fact Anglican registers, recording the marriages of individuals who were married 'according to the rites and ceremonies of the established Church'.

And don't forget that the marriages were also perfectly legal affairs. The problem with them is that they were so open to abuse, and by their very nature the registers are of questionable authenticity. There is evidence that details have been altered, names and dates changed and entirely false entries created. And it's also true to say that the records are difficult to use – some of them have been indexed but most remain effectively inaccessible – so a speculative search is a fairly desperate option. But you shouldn't ignore this source, as it has been estimated that perhaps half of all marriages in London in the 1740s and early 1750s took place in this way, in or around the Fleet Prison in London or at the Mayfair Chapel in Westminster. The surviving registers record around 350,000 marriages.

One rather surprising aspect of the Fleet Marriage Registers is that they also include a significant number of baptisms!

Roman Catholic records

The National Archives' collection of nonconformist records also includes a small number of Roman Catholic registers. There was significant resistance among the Catholic clergy to the General Register Office's registration commission and in the end only 77 congregations surrendered their registers. The bulk of these are from Yorkshire.

A detailed description of the history of Roman Catholicism in England and Wales is well beyond the scope of a book of this nature. But it is important to understand that for long periods between the English Reformation of 1534 and the passing of the Roman Catholic Relief Act in 1829, Catholicism was actively suppressed and its followers were sometimes ruthlessly persecuted. As a result of this persecution, Roman Catholics were understandably reluctant to record and publish records of their activities, which goes some way to explaining the relative scarcity of surviving records – particularly from the early years. Although many anti-Catholic laws remained in place, from 1689 onwards they were rarely enforced and Catholics were largely free to celebrate mass and perform baptisms.

There are several excellent sources which will help those of you with Catholic ancestors to locate the whereabouts of the surviving records. The most important of these is Michael Gandy's six-volume series *Catholic Missions and Registers 1700–1880* (details at the end of the book), which lists all known surviving Roman Catholic registers together with their covering dates and their current whereabouts.

Jewish records

The history of the Jews in England and Wales is even more problematical. The modern Jewish community in this country can trace its history back to the middle of the 17th century when Sephardic Jews (those from Italy, Spain and Portugal) started to arrive here, soon to be followed by Ashkenazim (from the Netherlands and Eastern Europe). The last few decades of the 19th century saw a huge influx of Jews from Russia and Poland. But since the births, marriages and deaths of our Jewish ancestors are fully covered by the General Register Office's civil registration process and Jewish families are recorded in the census returns in exactly the same way as the rest of the population, the modern records of these later immigrants are no different to those of our Anglican and nonconformist ancestors. Finding out exactly where in Eastern Europe they came from may be a difficult task, and one that is tied up with records of immigration and naturalization. Roger Kershaw and Mark Pearsall's book *Immigrants and Aliens* (details at the end of the book) is an excellent starting point for research in this area.

As a general rule, the records of the various Jewish communities in England and Wales are held by the relevant congregations. However, there are many records, including those of the Great Synagogue and the New Synagogue in London, which start as early as 1791, have been microfilmed and can be viewed at Latter-day Saints' family history centres. As has been mentioned before, Jews were exempted from the terms of Hardwicke's Marriage Act and therefore marriages which took place in the Jewish faith between 1754 and 1837 are legally valid.

The JewishGen website *www.jewishgen.org* is an excellent resource for Jewish family history. The site includes a searchable database which is rapidly growing into an invaluable tool for those with Jewish ancestry. The Jewish Genealogical Society of Great Britain is very active in promoting the use and understanding of specifically Jewish records in family history research. If you are serious about researching your own Jewish ancestors you should consider joining them.

Be prepared

These are probably the most important words that Scouts learn when they join their first troop, but the phrase is equally appropriate for family historians. If you're about to make your first trip to a record office or archive you really should prepare thoroughly for your visit.

First of all you need to know the basics about the office you're poised to descend on. What are its opening hours? Do you need to book in advance? Do you need to bring any identification with you? Does the archive actually have the records that you want to see and do you need to order anything in advance?

So many visits to record offices end up in disappointment simply because the researcher hasn't done their groundwork properly. Find out if you can obtain photocopies of the documents you're planning to look at. Do you need to bring a pencil? Unless it's the Family Records Centre in London that you're planning to visit, the answer to this question is definitely 'yes' — pens and archives just don't mix! Bags aren't welcome in reading rooms either, and most record offices provide lockers and a refreshment/cloakroom area — it's worth checking whether you need to bring a coin for the lockers.

And let's dispel straight away the image of archives as dark and dusty, oak-panelled, cobwebbed reading rooms, staffed by frightening, dusty, cobwebbed archivists. Most record offices these days are located in well-equipped, modern buildings with excellent facilities including state-of-the-art IT equipment. The staff are well trained, enthusiastic and friendly, and you'll find that many are active family historians themselves.

Don't be frightened of asking questions – even if you feel the question is too basic or trivial. Remember that the staff who work in record offices are only there because people like you and me want to use and understand the records in their care.

If you're travelling a long distance to get to the record office, particularly if you're not expecting to be able to go back regularly, you should do everything you can to ensure that you get the best out of your visit. Have a clear plan of what you want to achieve; make a list of the documents you want to see and find out what other records you might be able to look at while you're there.

The best source of all this information is the internet. Most record offices have very helpful sites and many of them have started to put their catalogues or indexes to their most important records online. The ARCHON directory at *www.national archives.gov.uk/archon* provides the contact details of all the record repositories in the United Kingdom and includes links to their own websites.

The more preparation you do, the more successful your day is likely to be. So don't get caught out – be prepared, and make the most of your day.

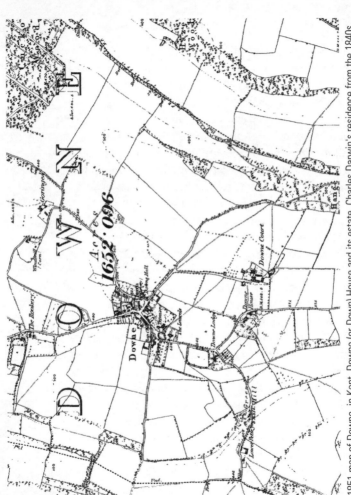

An 1851 map of Downe, in Kent. Downe (or Down) House and its estate, Charles Darwin's residence from the 1840s until his death, is shown to the south of the village itself.

Chapter 9

Picture this: the visual dimension

- Maps
- Prints and photographs

Maps and photographs are among the most important sources available to family historians, yet they are also among the most frequently ignored.

Maps

Maps come in all shapes and sizes and have been produced for a huge variety of reasons over the centuries. But there is no single central-ized collection of maps and there is no definitive list of what exists. Maps can be found in the records of countless government departments and regularly crop up in bundles of legal docu-ments, in the records of ecclesiastical and mano-rial courts and even among wills and census returns. Estate maps, transport maps showing roads, canals or railways, topographical maps and, of course, the extensive and varied collec-tion of plans published by the Ordnance Survey will help to place your ancestors' lives in their geographical context.

The National Archives has two collections of maps which are of particular value to family his-torians; both cover the whole of England and Wales. The earlier of these is the vast series of maps created by the Tithe Commission, which began work in 1836. The maps are accompanied by a series of 'apportionments', which are large, unwieldy documents that set out the names of the landowners and occupiers in each tithe district. They also record details of the various parcels of land, each of which is individually numbered, and it is these numbers which provide a link to the accompanying map and enable us to identify the whereabouts of the land and buildings owned or occupied by our ancestors.

Since most of the tithe maps date from around 1840, there is an obvious tie-in here with the 1841 census returns. Once you've found your ancestors in the census, a search of the relevant tithe documents should reveal exactly where they were living.

In addition to the (almost) complete collection held by the National Archives, you should find that most county record offices hold tithe records for their own area.

The other significant collection of maps held by the National Archives was created by the Valuation Office under the Finance Act (1909–10). The arrangement of the documents is very similar to that used by the Tithe Commission some seventy years earlier. A series of 'field books' is linked to thousands of heavily annotated maps of various scales. The scale of the map depended on the type of district being surveyed,

Did you know?

Until fairly recent times, the terms 'son-in-law' and 'daughter-in-law' were used where we would say 'step-son' or 'step-daughter'. If you find someone described in the census as the 'son-in-law' of the head of the household, he could either be the daughter's husband or the wife's son from a previous marriage.

with large-scale maps for the larger towns and cities and smaller scales for the rural areas.

As with the tithe apportionments, the field books contain details of the individual pieces of land. They also show the names of the occupiers and owners of the land as well as information about their liability for rates and taxes. Occasionally, sketch plans of individual properties are included. The records of this survey, commonly known as Lloyd George's Domesday, can shed light on a difficult period for family historians – a period before living memory (for most of us) but nearly a decade *after* the 1901 census.

Maps are a great way to understand how your ancestors' lives were affected and influenced by the areas where they lived. That family of yours from the small Suffolk coastal village would have led a very different sort of existence to that of your ancestors who lived on the North Yorkshire moors or in the valleys of South Wales. And the lives of the inhabitants of that remote hamlet on the edge of Dartmoor would have been poles apart from those of the family who lived in the little market town lying on the main road from London to Nottingham.

It's only by looking at contemporary maps of the areas that your ancestors lived in that you'll get a real feeling for all of this. The 1834 topographical maps published in *The Phillimore Atlas & Index of Parish Registers* are particularly useful as they show the country as it was just before the process of urbanization had really taken hold: a time when most of our ancestors still lived in rural areas. You can see at a glance whether your family's village was situated near a principal road; you can quickly identify the nearest major town – and don't ignore the waterways: rivers and canals were vital trade routes before the coming of the railways.

And remember that your ancestors wouldn't have worried too much about county boundaries, so if they lived near the edge of a county, don't forget to have a look at maps of the neighbouring areas.

Large-scale maps of the major towns and cities can help you to pinpoint the various addresses you've found in the census returns. And you can also use the maps to learn more about the areas where your ancestors lived. You can find the local churches and schools, the parks and cemeteries, the railway stations and tram routes, the factories and warehouses. The more detailed maps, showing the individual houses and gardens, will give you a good idea of the relative wealth of the area; large villas set in extensive gardens give a very different picture from the rows upon rows of terraced houses with their cramped backyards.

Prints and photographs

'What is the use of a book,' thought Alice, 'without pictures?' And the same is true of your research – after all, what is the use of a family history without pictures?

Wherever you find maps, you're also likely to find collections of prints, engravings and photographs. County record offices and local studies libraries often have large collections of visual material which you can use to illustrate your research and add an extra dimension to the story of your family.

With a bit of luck you might come across a photograph of the street that your ancestors lived in a hundred years ago. If not, then a view of the local high street will give you an idea of what the town was like, and if you discover nothing else you should at the very least be able to find an old print of the church where your great great grandparents were married. Most record offices will allow you to get copies from items in their photographic collections (for a fee) but don't forget to consider the copyright implications.

Old postcards are another way to illustrate your family's story. There are many companies which specialize in this area, and you'll often find them at family history fairs fighting for space with the local record offices and family history society stalls. You can also find hundreds of postcards for sale on websites such as eBay.

If you're thinking of publishing your family history (in printed form or on the internet) or if you just want to get a bit of additional background for your own personal interest, a good selection of prints and photographs, together with some photos from your own albums, will add a whole new dimension and really bring your research to life.

Putting flesh on the bones

The results of your family history research should be so much more than a long list of names and dates. Of course you need to do all the basics; you need to discover your ancestors' dates of birth, marriage and death and you need to know when their children were born, but ideally this should be a means to an end rather than an end in itself.

As a family historian you should look at a diverse range of sources including those that are traditionally thought of as sources for local history. In order to understand them better, you need to find out about the areas that your people came from. What were the main trades and industries? Who were the chief landowners and how did they influence your ancestors' lives? Was the population of the town on the increase or declining? When did the railways arrive and what effect did this have on the town?

And the chances are that the answers to these questions have already been researched and published. There can't be a town or city in England and Wales which hasn't been the subject of at least one major historical study, and you'll probably find that several have been published over the years. Even quite small villages are likely to have something on offer.

Local studies libraries are an excellent source for this sort of material, and you should also find that they have good collections of earlier county histories in which 18th- and 19th-century historians looked at the history of their counties from the perspective of the major landowners. Although these might seem to have little relevance to those of us with ancestors who worked on the land rather than owned it, it's always worthwhile finding out what they have to say about your ancestors' parish – you never know what you might discover.

Social, political and even national history are also areas that you should investigate. Your ancestors may not have taken part in the Captain Swing Riots of 1830 and they may not have been among the crowd at St Peter's Field, Manchester, in 1819 to witness the Peterloo Massacre, but if they lived through these times they would certainly have been affected by the events. If any of your ancestors were agricultural labourers living in southern England in 1830, the social and economic factors that led to the Swing Riots and the transportation of the Tolpuddle Martyrs a few years later would have been of enormous importance to them, and it's therefore likely that they would have had strong opinions on the issues of the day.

Similarly, the Chartist movement of the 1830s and 1840s had a huge impact on the lives of ordinary people. Over three million people signed a petition, which was presented to Parliament in 1842. This document demanded the introduction of universal male suffrage – at this stage, even most Chartists felt that votes for women was a step too far. The petition was rejected but the campaign continued, and it's not at all unlikely that your ancestors may have been actively involved.

The English Civil War touched the lives of practically everyone who lived in the middle of the 17th century. Again, your ancestors may not have been involved in any of the pitched battles or sieges, and they may not have had particularly strong Royalist or Parliamentarian views themselves, but they can hardly fail to have been affected by the conflict in some way or other.

The most important thing to remember here is that the names on your family tree relate to real people: people with real hopes and fears; people who would have been devastated by the early death of their youngest son just as they were overjoyed by the birth of their first grandchild; people who lived through dramatic national and local events. Foreign wars and the failure of a crop would equally have affected their lives.

So when you come across that single line in the parish register recording your ancestor's baptism, don't just make a note of the date and move quickly on to the next item on your list. Instead, try to imagine the baby wrapped in her christening robes as the vicar holds her over the font and her parents look on, happy but a little anxious. Picture the same parents twenty years on, as they proudly watch their daughter walking up the aisle to start a new life with the blacksmith's son, who they've known since he was a baby. And then the sad scene at the graveside in the churchyard of the same parish church as, through tear-filled eyes, the young woman sees her father's coffin lowered into the ground, with her own children gathered beside her.

Family history isn't a scientific pursuit, it's a voyage of discovery, and your aim should be to learn as much as you can about your ancestors and to find out what their lives were really like.

A LIST of BIRTHS for the Year 1744.

SEPT. 2. THE Countess of *Carlisle*, delivered of a Daughter, at *Castle Howard* in *Yorkshire*.

10. The Wife of *Barnaby Backwell*, Esq; Banker at *Temple-bar*,——of a Son.

13. The Lady of the Hon. *Edw. Boscawen*, Capt. of the *Dreadnought*,——of a Son.

17. The Wife of *Peregrine Bertie*, Esq;——of a Son.

Alderman *Baker*'s Lady,——of a Son.

26. The Wife of *Nicholas Corsellis* of *Wivenhoe*, *Essex*, Esq;——of a Son and Heir.

A LIST of MARRIAGES for the Year 1744

Aug. 25. MR *Lee*, an eminent Surgeon at *Mile-end*, was married at St Paul's, to Miss *Molly Harrison* of *Clerkenwell*.

Mr *Prescot*, Master of *Catherine-hall*, *Cambridge*, and Prebendary of *Norwich*,——to Miss *Appleyard*.

SEPT. 1. Mr *Josiah Colvil*, an eminent Hop-merchant in *Watling-street*,——to Miss *Dodd* of *Stepney*.

4. Col. *Cunningham*,——to Miss *Meerrick*, with 50000 *l*. Fortune.

7. Mr *Woodhouse*, an eminent Attorney in *Fleetstreet*,——to Miss *Baylis*, with 5,000 *l*.

11. Sam. *Shephard* of *Blisworth*, *Northamptonsh*. Esq;——to Miss *Sheppard* of *Southwark*.

15. Gen. *Oglethorpe*,——to the only Daughter of the late Sir *Nathan Wright*, Bt, of *Cransham Hall*, *Essex*. (*Erase this Gent. &c.* p. 451.)

20. The Rev. Doctor *Gibson*, Son to the Bp of *London*,——to a Niece of Lady *Hopkin*'s.

Payne King, Esq; Heir to Dr *King*, late Master of the *Charter-house*,——to one of the Daughters of *James Colebrooke*, Esq;

21. Mr *Abraham Henckell*, an eminent *Hamburgh* Merchant in *Cannon-street*,——to Miss *Cornwall* of *Rotherhithe*.

Sir *Rich. Acton*, Bt,——to Lady *Anne Gray*.

MARRIAGES at Dublin.

18. Mr Justice *York* of the *Common-pleas*,——to the Widow *Cope*; Niece to Ld ch. J. *Singleton*.

Vesey Colcclough, Esq;——to Mrs *Montgomery*.

John Ong, Esq; Counsellor at Law,——to Miss *Callan*, with 10,000 *l*.

A LIST of DEATHS for the Year 1744.

Aug. 31. Capt. *John Scott*, formerly in the

mander in the *Spanish* and *West India* Trade,

Mr *Percival*, an eminent Sugar Baker.

Mr *Banks*, an eminent Merchant, at *Borne*.

12. *George Proctor*, Esq; at *Epsom*.

Mrs *Lesteck*, at the Admiral's in *Chigwell*.

Ld *Critchton*, only Son to the E. of *Dauphin*.

15. The Wife of *Hercules Baker*, Esq; Member of Parliament for *Hythe*; at *Deal* in *Kent*.

17. *James Thompson*, Esq; of *Lewis* in *Sussex*.

21. *Thomas Gibson*, Esq; an eminent Money Scrivener, in *Lothbury*, and Member of Parliament for *Yarmouth*, *Hants*.

At *Bath*, *William Nevil*, Lord *Abergaveny*, first Baron of *England*, and Master of the Jewel-Office.

24. Mr *West*, Ship-builder, at *Deptford*, worth 30,000 *l*.

A LIST of PROMOTIONS for the Year 1744

CAPT. *Taylor*, made Captain of the *Foward* a 20 Gun-ship, lately built at *Hull*.

Capt. *Gordon*,——of the *Sheerness*, in room of

Capt. *Rodney*,——of the *Ludlow-Castle*, 40 G.

In the 2d Troop of GUARDS,

Capt. *Mutlow*, made Adjutant, in room of

Capt. *Scudder*,——Brigadier, in room of

Capt. *Brattle*,——eldest Exempt, in room of

Capt. *Clarke*,——Major, in room of Major *Edwards*, decd.

Capt. *Decerney*,——Major of Horse Grenadier Guards, in room of

Major *Ferth*,——Lieut. Col. of Dragoons, in room of Col. *Cunningham*, res.

ECCLESIASTICAL PREFERMENTS, conferred on the following Rev. Gentlemen.

MR *Wilson*, Fellow of *Catherine Hall*, *Cambridge*, collated by the Bp of *London*, to the Rectory of *Halstead*, *Essex*.

Mr *Christopher Wilson*, presented to the Rect. of *Willing*, *Essex*.

Mr *George Jaques*, made a Preb. of *Wells*,

Mr *Ibbetson*,——a Preacher at *Whitehall*.

BANKRUPTS.

Chapter 10

Read all about it: newspapers

- Newspapers and family history
- Newspaper collections
- A magazine of note
- The whole truth?

Newspapers have been with us now for over three hundred years, but it wasn't until the late Victorian era brought about the growth of adult literacy that they really became such an important part of everyday life for most people in England and Wales.

Newspapers and family history

As a source for family history research they are unrivalled and incomparable. And they all have a contribution to make to our research, from the national broadsheets like *The Times*, *The Daily Telegraph* and *The Guardian* with their comprehensive coverage of national and international events to the early 19th-century 'county' journals – which also tended to cover national news but with a slight local flavour to it – right down to the thousands of local newspapers which appeared in the middle of the 19th century and, as the years progressed, began to focus more and more on genuinely local news.

Newspapers have much to offer the family historian, but as with so many of these useful sources, if you want to get the best out of them you'll probably need to prepare yourself for a lot of long and occasionally frustrating searching. Carrying out a speculative search in your local newspaper is unlikely to produce anything worth-while. You really need to have the date of a spe-cific event in mind and you need to consider whether the event is likely to have been covered by the paper. And don't forget that there may have been more than one local newspaper for your area – it was not at all uncommon to find two or more rival publications operating in the same town, often representing different political interests.

Even in Victorian times, most local newspa-pers provided columns where for a small fee people could announce the births, marriages and deaths of their nearest and dearest, but while these announcements can be quite useful to us they are unlikely to reveal anything startlingly interesting. Having said that, occasionally you may stumble across the announcement of the death of an uncle who emigrated to New Zealand fifty years ago or the birth of a child who was pre-viously unknown to you.

Some papers published quite extensive reports on local weddings, particularly if the cou-ple getting married happened to be the children of local dignitaries. If you're lucky enough to find a report like this, you may get some very useful information from the guest lists which often accompanied the report.

It's in the areas relating to deaths that local newspapers really come into their own. The Victorian fascination with reading the reports of inquests has already been mentioned but bears repeating – they really are an important source, particularly as the original coroner's reports may have been destroyed or may still be 'closed'. Whenever you see the words 'coroner' or 'inquest' on a death certificate you should look for a report in the relevant local newspaper.

And if your ancestor was a person of any standing in the town, it is well worth checking the local newspapers for the week or two after his death. A good, thorough, well-researched obituary can be worth its weight in gold. You may learn when and where your ancestor was born and where he was educated; you may discover that he served in the Army and was awarded a medal for bravery; he may have been a member of the town council or a senior trade unionist, or perhaps he was a prominent local sportsman and captained the local cricket eleven. If you're lucky you might even find a picture of him accompanying the report.

If you do find something like this, don't stop there. It's quite likely that the following week's paper will include a report of his funeral together with a list of the mourners. Not only will this add

Did you know?

If your ancestor was a 'journeyman tailor' or a 'journey-man blacksmith', don't be fooled into thinking that this meant that he travelled around the country as part of his job. The term 'journeyman' describes someone who has served an apprenticeship in a particular trade or handicraft and is now working for someone else. His employer would be a 'master' of his trade.

to your knowledge of the family but now that you know where he was buried you have a whole new source to investigate.

If your ancestor was a tradesman or shop-keeper it's possible that he may have advertised his services in the local newspaper. Many of these adverts were highly decorative works of art in their own right, and for the family historian they can add an interesting visual aspect to your documentary research.

Local and national newspapers regularly publish legal announcements from solicitors asking people to contact them if they believe they are related to a person who has recently died, leaving behind a substantial sum of money but no will. The significance of this sort of announcement is obvious to family historians, but be warned that if the inspiration behind your research is the thought of discovering a long-lost family fortune you are almost certain to be disappointed!

As with the sources we looked at in the last chapter, newspapers can also be used to colour the background of your ancestors' lives. The report of a fatal accident in a mine in South Wales is the story of an event that would have affected not just the miner and his family but the whole local community. The contemporary reports of the death and funeral of Queen Victoria, for example, illustrate just how our ancestors' lives were influenced and shaped by these local and national events; and newspapers can help us to understand exactly what in these events was important to them.

Newspaper collections

The British Library Newspapers collection at Colindale comprises over 50,000 titles dating from 1699 up to the present day – a total of 664,000 bound volumes and over 370,000 reels of microfilm. The bulk of the collection relates to newspapers published in the United Kingdom and the Republic of Ireland but there are also large numbers of foreign titles, including many from Western Europe and the former British colonies. The Newspaper Library has an extensive collection of journals and periodicals so if, for example, your ancestor was involved in a trade or had an active interest in a particular sport or hobby it might be worth investigating whether there's a relevant publication that would help you to find out more about him. The British Library's online newspaper catalogue currently lists over 50,000 titles.

Local studies libraries usually have copies of the newspapers that were published in their own areas of interest and many have collections of cuttings with card indexes.

Some large libraries have copies of *The Times* on microfilm, and although it is unlikely that most ordinary people will ever have been mentioned in this venerable old publication, the existence of an index both in printed form and online (The Times Digital Archive) means that a speculative search for your ancestors is quite a feasible option.

A magazine of note

During the 18th and 19th centuries a number of periodicals were published which may have some value for family historians. The most important of these was *The Gentleman's Magazine* which was founded in 1731 and ran until 1914. Although most of the pages were taken up with literary criticism, essays and parliamentary reports, there was also a regular births, marriages and deaths section which is well indexed. Admittedly, the majority of these entries relate to the more rich and famous members of society, but considering that at its peak it had a circulation figures of over 10,000 readers, *The Gentleman's Magazine* is a potentially valuable source for all family historians.

The whole truth?

Before we leave newspapers, a word of warning. Almost all of us, at some time in our lives, will have come into contact with the local press. Perhaps you scored the winning goal for your school team or you were involved in a car accident; maybe you were a witness to a street theft or you gave a talk to your local women's group. It's a pretty safe bet that when you saw the article in the paper the following week, you found that at least one detail was incorrect or that something in the report was slightly inaccurate. This is not intended to be a criticism of journalists, local or otherwise; after all, we already know that we shouldn't believe everything we read in the papers.

Nevertheless, as family historians it's important that we always remember this when we're reading reports of our ancestors' activities and, as with other sources that we use in the course of our research, we should always ask questions and never take 'facts' on trust.

Digging around

By the time you've searched all the 19th-century census returns for your ancestors' village, spent hours
trawling through the parish registers and poured
over an assortment of local maps, you'll start to feel
that you've really got to know the place. But there's
no substitute for making a personal visit to the
areas that your ancestors knew so well.

If they came from a small town or village you
might be lucky and discover that not much has
changed. The church is still there with the almshous-
es next to it; the old inn on the village green is still
serving food and drink and the village store is open
for business. You may even find that the house your
family lived in hundreds of years ago is still standing
and in good repair, and you can let yourself imagine
the barefooted children running out of the back door,
along the lane and across the fields.

Some of the older residents may have known your
family, and if you let them know why you're visiting
the village they may relish the opportunity to get
talking about the past. The owner of the local stores
will probably be able to tell you the best people to
talk to about the history of the village.

Of course, you'll want to spend some time walking
around the churchyard, and naturally you'll be hoping
to find some family gravestones. Take your time and

look carefully at each of the stones — just as when you're looking through a parish register, you can easily miss something important if you rush these things. Strong sunlight will help you to read the more difficult inscriptions but if they're covered in moss, ivy or lichen there may be nothing you can do. You should seek permission and expert advice before attempting to clean any stones as you may actually do more harm than good.

Some types of stone do not cope well with the wet English winters and can become badly decayed after a hundred years or so, and some may have fallen over, face down, making them impossible to read. You should never attempt to lift a fallen stone — graveyards can be dangerous places if you don't take sensible precautions. And don't forget that there may be quite recent burials next to the graves of your long-dead ancestors — think about where you're walking and treat all graves with respect and consideration.

Even in the more developed areas, there's a lot to be said for spending some time exploring the neighbourhood. The old houses may have gone and the street layout may have changed beyond recognition but many of the features that your ancestors knew are probably still there — the churches, the parks, the schools and the town hall, for instance.

If you're spending a few days in the area, you

should take the opportunity to visit the appropriate local studies library. They are often understaffed and under-resourced and their opening times may be quite limited, but they are a wonderful source, and one of the main reasons that they don't receive the funding they so badly need is that they are not used enough. Their collections of local material are unique and irreplaceable and the staff who work there probably have an expert knowledge of the area. You may have to make an appointment to use the facilities, so make sure that you plan your trip a good time in advance.

One of the most useful tools you can take with you on these excursions into the past is a camera. Think of it as your opportunity to make a record for future generations of what the area looked like when you went walking in your ancestors' footsteps — but remember to date the photographs.

An Extract from an Entry in the Army War Records of Deaths 1914-1921

CERTIFIED COPY OF   AN ENTRY OF **DEATH**

SA 066559

Application Number GB01234

Registration of Births, Deaths and Marriages (Special Provisions) Act 1957

Army Officers Records of War Deaths 1914 - 1921

Name and Rank	Unit	Cause, Date and Place of Death
DARWIN E. 2nd Lt.	4 Bn. Yorkshire Regiment T.F.	Killed in Action, 25.4.1915, France or Belgium

An Extract from an Entry relating to the death of Erasmus Darwin

CERTIFIED to be a true copy of the *certified copy of* an entry made in a Service Departments Register.

Given at the GENERAL REGISTER OFFICE, under the Seal of the said Office, the 12th day of **September 2005**

Section VI(3) of the above mentioned Act provides that "No extractiness relating to the registration of births, and deaths and marriages in England and Wales, Scotland and Northern Ireland which contain provisions authorising the admission in evidence of, any of extracts from, certified copies of registers and duplicate registers) shall have effect as if the Service Departments Registers were certified copies or duplicate registers transmitted to the Registrar General in accordance with those enactments.

CAUTION: THERE ARE OFFENCES RELATING TO FALSIFYING OR ALTERING A CERTIFICATE AND USING OR POSSESSING A FALSE CERTIFICATE

CROWN COPYRIGHT

WARNING: A CERTIFICATE IS NOT EVIDENCE OF IDENTITY.

A certified copy of an entry of death for Erasmus Darwin (Charles Darwin's grandson), killed in action in 'France or Belgium', 25 April 1914.

Chapter 11

The bigger picture: the British Isles and abroad

- Scotland
- Ireland
- The Channel Islands and the Isle of Man
- Births, marriages and deaths at sea and overseas
- Emigration
- Immigration

Up to now, this book has concerned itself largely with the records used to trace English and Welsh ancestors. In itself, this is fine if your ancestors happened to spend the whole of their lives in these lands, without setting foot on foreign soil. Of course, the population has never been that settled, and it's highly likely that even among your English or Welsh relatives some of them will have migrated during the course of their lives – within the British Isles, across the Channel to the European continent, over the Atlantic Ocean or even further afield to India and the Far East. And the other side of the coin is that your own ancestors may have moved from another country in order to settle here.

So in this chapter we'll consider the British Isles more generally, as well as the millions of people who have left these shores to start new lives in Australia, South Africa, New Zealand, the Americas and elsewhere. We'll also look at those immigrants who have arrived over the centuries: from countries such as France, Italy, Germany, Poland and Russia, and, more recently, from the Indian sub-continent, Africa and the Caribbean. Much of this movement has been of people seeking refuge from political or religious persecution, but perhaps just as many of the individuals have been tradespeople, artisans, craftsmen or

Did you know?

Significant immigration from the Caribbean began when colonial service personnel stayed on in Britain after the Second World War. Immigration was then encouraged from 1948 to solve postwar labour shortages and alleviate unemployment in the West Indies. When the labour market reached a surplus, the 1962 Commonwealth Immigrants Act began the process of restricting entry.

other kinds of economic migrants in search of opportunities to earn a decent living.

We also need to consider what we might call 'temporary migrants' – people who travelled overseas, spent some time away, and then returned. They may have been working or simply travelling abroad, or perhaps they were 'serious' emigrants who decided after a few years that life in the new country wasn't for them and set out on the long voyage back home – and this happened more frequently than you might expect.

Before we look at how to trace records of migrant ancestors, let's start a bit closer to home by looking at the other parts of the British Isles. While these are not 'foreign' lands in the same sense, it's important to bear in mind that for family history research they are distinct: Scotland, Ireland, the Channel Islands and the Isle of Man have always kept their own records. But even if you consider yourself of English or Welsh ancestry, it's likely there is some Irish or Scottish blood somewhere along the line, so in any event it's a good idea to become familiar with the basic sources in these areas.

Scotland

The records that we use for researching our Scottish ancestors are essentially the same as we would use in England and Wales. However, the civil registration records of births, marriages and deaths provide family historians with some valuable additional information. The downside is that registration didn't start in Scotland until 1 January 1855 but this is more than made up for by the extra details that were recorded.

In addition to the information shown on English and Welsh birth certificates, their Scottish equivalents record:

- the time of birth
- the date and place of the parents' marriage

In the early years of civil registration in Scotland even more information was requested, but this level of detail turned out to be unsustainable. In 1855, the following additional details were recorded:

- the father's age and birthplace
- his previous issue, living and deceased (numbers and sex only)
- the mother's age and birthplace

This was quickly abandoned and these three questions, along with the date and place of the parents' marriage, were absent from birth certificates between 1856 and 1860. In 1861 this last item was reinstated.

It's not hard to see how useful this extra information is, providing as it does a direct link between birth and marriage certificates wholly absent in England and Wales.

Scottish marriage certificates record one additional (and extremely useful) piece of information: namely, the names and maiden surnames of the mothers. They also include a specific question asking whether the parents of the bridegroom and the bride are deceased, and, as with births, there were some extra items in the early years that were soon abandoned:

- if a widower or a widow, whether second or third marriage (1855 only)
- children by each former marriage (numbers living and dead) (1855 only)
- the relationship of parties (if related) (1855 to 1860)

Since 1972, Scottish marriage certificates have recorded the bride and bridegroom's dates of birth rather than their ages.

Unlike their English and Welsh counterparts, Scottish death certificates are simply packed with additional information, including:

- the marital status of the deceased
- their father's name, occupation and whether *he* is deceased
- their mother's name (including maiden surname) and whether *she* is deceased
- their spouse's name (including maiden surname where relevant)

Again, the early years of death registration saw an abundance of extra questions:

- the deceased's place of birth (1855 only)
- how long they had lived in the district in which they died (1855 only)
- the names and ages (at date of death certificate) of their children *or* the age and year of death if the child pre-deceased their parent (1855 only)
- their burial place (1855 to 1860)

Unfortunately, the registrars soon found that all this was simply too much and that in many cases the informants were unable to provide the information they required with any degree of accuracy. And this is also a matter to consider with later Scottish death certificates – if a young man is registering his grandfather's death, how likely is he to have known his grandfather's mother's maiden surname?

But despite this, it's pretty clear that all of this extra information on Scottish certificates is a real boon to those of us with ancestors from north of the border, making the difficult task of identifying individuals in the records, and building bridges from generation to generation, that much easier.

Scottish censuses are no different, in terms of content, to the returns for England and Wales. The dates of the censuses are the same, the layout of the forms is almost identical and the same basic questions were asked.

Scottish parish registers, on the other hand, tend not to have been so well kept as their English counterparts. The earliest surviving register dates from 1553 but in the more remote areas, particularly in the Highlands and Islands, many of the registers don't start until the early 1800s.

Although you stand a good chance of finding a complete run of baptismal and marriage registers for your ancestors' parish from the mid 1600s, burial registers are frequently lacking. Baptismal registers normally record the date of birth, and where burial registers survive they usually show the date of death.

Parish registers almost always record women's maiden names, so that a typical entry in a baptismal register might start:

> *Isabel, lawful daughter of James Hunter and Catherine Miller ...*

The word 'lawful' indicates that James and Catherine were married and that the birth was therefore legitimate. The word 'natural' was used to indicate an illegitimate birth.

Scottish parish registers are commonly referred to as Old Parish Registers (OPRs).

Wills and testaments in Scotland work in a slightly different way to those in England and Wales. A testament is a legal document that allows an executor to administer the deceased's estate. There were two types of testament: a *testament testamentar* was issued by the courts when the deceased had left a will, naming an executor; and, when the deceased died intestate (without leaving a will), an executor could be appointed by the court and would be issued with a *testament dative*. Records survive from the early 1500s but it's fair to say that, over the years, only a very small proportion of Scots have left wills.

There can be no doubt that as a family historian it pays to be Scottish. We've already looked at some of the extra details recorded on the major sources, but another huge advantage of using Scottish records is that women tended to keep their maiden surnames for most legal purposes; so not only in parish registers, but also in wills and testaments, and on gravestones, you should expect to see women's maiden names used as a matter of course – you may even come across this practice on some of the earlier census returns.

And there are two other great benefits of having Scottish ancestors: first, all of the birth, marriage and death certificates, the census returns and the parish registers are located in the same building in Edinburgh – New Register House, the home of the General Register Office for Scotland – and the old wills and testaments are located next door at the National Archives of Scotland.

Second, and even more important for those unfortunate enough not to be able to travel to Edinburgh, the vast majority of these records are now available online, fully indexed and linked to digital images of the original documents. And better still, they can all be accessed on one site – ScotlandsPeople: *www.scotlandspeople.gov.uk*

The site provides access to the following:

- births (1855–1904)
- marriages (1855–1929)
- deaths (1855–1954)
- baptisms (OPRs) (1553–1854) (images not available
- marriages (OPRs) (1553–1854) (images not available)
- 1871 census
- 1881 census (images not available)
- 1891 census
- 1901 census
- wills and testaments (1513–1901)

There are also records of Scottish 'overseas' births, marriages and deaths (including war deaths) from 1855, and all of this is available on a pay-per-view basis, worldwide, twenty-four hours a day, with more to follow in 2005/2006 including the remaining censuses back to 1841 and the images of the OPRs.

The National Archives of Scotland holds a vast range of sources relating to land ownership, the Poor Law, nonconformist congregations, emigration and taxation as well as over five hundred years' worth of records from the Court of Sessions and other courts of law.

Although the most important sources are

centralized in these two remarkable repositories situated next door to each other in Edinburgh, there is a wealth of useful material available in local record offices and libraries the length and breadth of Scotland, such as Glasgow's Mitchell Library and the city archives of Dundee and Aberdeen, to name but a few. Indeed, as in England and Wales, practically every major town in Scotland has a local studies centre that would be well worth visiting if your ancestors have come from that area.

Ireland

The situation in Ireland is somewhat less favourable for family historians, partly because so much of the basic source material has not survived, and partly because almost none of the primary source material is available online.

Irish family history has suffered two great losses: one caused by a fire in Dublin during the civil war in 1922, and the other the result of wholesale destruction by the Irish government.

A full census return of the whole of Ireland had been taken every ten years since 1821, and from 1861 a question was included about religious denomination. It's possible that the sensitive nature of this question may have led to the unfortunate decision to destroy the returns for 1861, 1871, 1881 and 1891. Whatever the reason, the absence of this major source has left a gaping hole for Irish researchers. But worse was to come.

By 1922, the earlier census returns had been deposited with the Public Record Office (the forerunner of The National Archives of Ireland) and when a fire broke out that year at the Four Courts building in Dublin, they were tragically lost, along with countless other irreplaceable documents. The implications for Irish family history are enormous. Not only are there almost no surviving Victorian censuses (a few small fragments survived), but it has been estimated that around half of the Church of Ireland's parish registers also perished in the fire. When you add to this the loss of almost all Irish probate records from before 1858 as well as a huge collection of legal material and medieval statute rolls, you begin to get an idea of how catastrophic the fire was for the study of Irish history in general.

But it's not all bad news. The civil registration records, which start in 1864, were held by the General Register Office for Ireland and were therefore unaffected by the fire. The 1901 and 1911 censuses (which were also held by the GRO at the time) have survived in full and are now held by the National Archives in Dublin where they can be viewed on microfilm. The National Library of Ireland holds a large collection of Roman Catholic parish registers, and the surviving records of the Church of Ireland and those of the various nonconformist congregations such as the Presbyterians, Methodists and Baptists are also extremely valuable sources. However, there is no central location for these church registers and tracking down records for a particular townland or parish may involve visits to a number of different repositories. *The Irish Times* has an excellent website called Irish Ancestors at *www.ireland.com/ancestor*, which gives some useful pointers on tracking down the surviving records.

A number of 'census substitutes' are available and go some way towards making up for the almost complete lack of official returns. The most important of these is Griffith's Valuation, an extensive listing of the names of the occupiers and owners of land throughout Ireland from 1845 onwards. The records of Griffith's Valuation are now available online at *www.irishorigins.com*.

Irish civil registration records are practically identical in terms of layout and content to those of England and Wales. And although the full registration service started in 1864 (much later than elsewhere in the UK), it's important to note that registration of non-Catholic marriages began nearly twenty years earlier in 1845 – this is a significant source which should not be overlooked. Records of births, marriages and deaths in Ireland are held by the General Register Office for Ireland in Dublin.

As with other parts of the British Isles, Ireland has a vast range of useful local sources and is particularly fortunate to have the resources of a network of local heritage centres where you can get expert advice and guidance on researching your Irish ancestors.

From 1922, records relating to Northern Ireland are held separately. The Public Record Office of Northern Ireland (PRONI) has copies of the 1901 census returns (but not 1911) while civil registration records for Northern Ireland are held by the General Register Office (Northern Ireland). Registers of births and deaths from 1864 and marriages from 1922 can be searched on computerized indexes at the General Register Office in Belfast.

The Channel Islands and the Isle of Man

Jersey, Guernsey (including Alderney and Sark) and the Isle of Man have never been part of the

United Kingdom as far as civil registration is concerned. All have their own register offices, archives and libraries, with records of births, marriages and deaths, parish registers and wills as well as significant collections of legal documents and records of local taxation and land ownership.

The census returns for these islands are included with the returns for England and Wales. You can see them at the Family Records Centre on microfilm or online as part of the Ancestry and 1901 Census Online websites. Copies are also held in the relevant local archives.

The GENUKI website is an excellent source of information about the vast range of material that is available for both the Channel Islands and the Isle of Man.

Births, marriages and deaths at sea and overseas

As well as attempting to perform the unenviable task of recording every birth, marriage and death to have taken place in England and Wales since July 1837, the General Register Office has responsibility for registering events relating to English and Welsh citizens that took place overseas and at sea.

The records created by this ongoing process form a vast and diverse collection of registers, which includes:

- births, marriages and deaths registered by the British Forces and the British Consul or High Commission in the country where they took place, from 1849;
- deaths that occurred in the Boer War and both world wars;
- British Army regimental records of births, baptisms and marriages dating back to 1761;
- marine births and deaths, from 1837, which took place on British registered vessels;
- aircraft births and deaths, from 1948, which took place on British registered aircraft.

These registers are by no means a comprehensive record of all such events and they do not, as a rule, include records of births, marriages and deaths which took place in Commonwealth countries such as Australia, Canada, New Zealand, South Africa or the Indian sub-continent. Nor do they record events relating to permanent emigrants, so the marriage or death of your ancestor's brother who emigrated to Argentina in the 1870s are unlikely to be found here. In each of these cases, events involving British citizens would have been registered locally and the British authorities would have considered them perfectly valid for all legal purposes.

Nevertheless, the 'overseas' registers do contain many thousands of records of English and Welsh citizens whose births, marriages and deaths were registered at a British embassy or on board a British vessel, and they also contain records of servicemen and women and their families who were stationed overseas.

The registers also include records of war deaths, with the registers of British soldiers who died in World War I representing a significant proportion of them. The certificates themselves contain very little information of real interest to family historians and often give the soldier's place of death as simply 'France' or 'Flanders', but they do show the age and date of death, along with the man's name, rank and number, so they can be a useful starting point for further research into an ancestor's military service records.

Each of these sources is indexed separately and it wasn't until 1969 that the GRO started to compile single annual indexes to all registered overseas events. The indexes are held by the Family Records Centre but they are also available on microfiche in a number of record offices and libraries around the country, and you can search them online at *www.1837online.com*.

The National Archives also holds a large amount of overseas material, which family historians would find extremely useful if only they knew of its existence. Now known as the 'Miscellaneous Overseas Registers', this assorted collection of registers was originally transferred from the General Register Office in the 1970s. These are largely non-statutory records of births (and baptisms), marriages, deaths (and burials) of British subjects which took place overseas and at sea. The collection includes a number of registers from former British protectorates in Africa and Asia, and the oldest volume in the series is a register from The Hague which was started in 1627. More records are added periodically, and the most recent dates from 1969.

The GRO's marine registers are complemented by another source held by the National Archives at Kew: the records of the Registrar General of Shipping and Seamen. These are mainly duplicates of the GRO's registers but are well worth searching for additional entries which may not have been forwarded to the relevant General Register Office.

Another large collection of overseas registers of baptisms, marriages and burials, formerly held by the Bishop of London, can now be searched at London's Guildhall Library.

The British Library in London is home to a remarkable collection of material compiled by the

British authorities in India between 1600 and 1947. Registers of the baptisms, marriages and burials of Anglo-Indians in the various Presidencies of Bengal (from 1713), Madras (from 1698) and Bombay (from 1709) are among the archives that were transferred to the British Library following Indian independence in 1947, along with volumes of wills, records of the Indian Army and Navy, and civil service appointment books. If your ancestor was one of the thousands of English men and women included in these records, you're likely to discover some surprising details about their lives in British India.

All of these sources are worth investigating and you can find out more about them in *Tracing Your Ancestors in the National Archives* by Amanda Bevan and *The British Overseas* published by Guildhall Library.

Emigration

As we have seen, Scotland and Ireland have always had their own legal systems (which led to the creation of their own distinct records). However, the Acts of Union of 1707 (with Scotland) and 1800 (with Ireland) saw the various parts of the British Isles joining together to form a single state. And this was to mean that movement from Glasgow to Belfast, from Cork to Bristol or from Manchester to Edinburgh did not constitute emigration (or immigration, for that matter) any more than moving from Durham to Liverpool did – it was simply a case of migrating from one place to another within the same nation-state. So don't expect to find any records of your Irish 'immigrant' ancestor's arrival in England – he wasn't an immigrant and his journey from Roscommon wouldn't have resulted in the creation of any sort of documentation.

Tracing records of people who moved further afield is, unfortunately, rarely an easy task. And your best chance of finding any surviving documentation of their movement is amongst the records of the country of arrival. The British government was not terribly concerned about people leaving these shores, whereas the authorities in Australia, for example, kept very good records. However, the National Archives in Kew does hold a wide variety of records relating to emigration:

- passenger lists for ships leaving the United Kingdom (1890 to 1960)
- registers of convicts transported to Australia (1787 to 1868)
- Colonial Office records of correspondence (1817 to 1896)

- Poor Law Union papers concerning assisted emigration schemes (1834–90)
- Foreign Office passport registers (1795 to 1898)

Other sources include Plantation Books, Privy Council Registers, Colonial State Papers and the records of various child migration schemes (mainly to Canada) between 1869 and 1930.

These records contain thousands of files and registers, including references to thousands, possibly even millions of people who left the UK to settle in other countries around the world. The problem with using this material is that hardly any of it is indexed and your chances of finding anything about a particular individual are somewhat remote.

The Society of Genealogists has what is possibly the UK's best collection of material relating to British emigrants. Much of this is printed material, published in the countries where the emigrants ended up. Probably the most important of these are the volumes of ships' passenger lists, recording the names (and sometimes the ages and places of origin) of emigrants to the United States and Canada from the 1500s. These are by no means comprehensive lists of such emigrants, but they do contain many thousands of names and there's a good chance of finding a distant relative listed here.

Immigration

In the past few years a huge amount of effort has gone into making the records of people settling in the British Isles more accessible. And the results of this work can now be found on a website called Moving Here at *www.movinghere.org.uk.* The site provides access to original documents relating to immigration and also includes photographs and personal stories. Moving Here concentrates on the Caribbean, Irish, Jewish and South Asian communities in Britain over the past 200 years, but there are plans to cover other immigrant groups in the future.

It's important to remember that once an immigrant arrived in this country, they would be treated in the same way as anyone else as far as civil registration, census returns and probate records are concerned.

For many of us, the first clue that we have an immigrant ancestor may come from an unexpected birthplace on a census return. The census enumerators' instructions were to give just the country of birth, but if you're lucky you might get the name of a particular town or village, which will give you an excellent lead for further research in the native country.

Many immigrants soon adopted 'anglicized' versions of their names; this is a particular problem with Jewish immigrants arriving from Eastern Europe in the latter half of the 19th century and it can provide you with almost insurmountable difficulties. In English law, people are free to call themselves by any name they choose, providing they're not doing so for fraudulent purposes. Very few people who changed their names did so officially, by deed poll, and of those who did, only a small percentage chose to have the record of their change of name 'enrolled'. So it's best not to hold out too much hope of finding anything here.

As with the records of emigration that we looked at above, the best sources for information about your immigrant ancestors are held by the National Archives. The most important records are:

- records of denizations and naturalizations (1500s to 1936)
- passenger lists (1878 to 1960)
- certificates of aliens (1836 to 1852)
- entry books (1794 to 1909)
- changes of name by deed poll (to 1997)

Several early series of records among the State Papers and Chancery Rolls also include references to immigrant communities in Britain.

You should be warned that these documents may promise more than they actually deliver, as the fact is that the records held by the National Archives record only a very small percentage of people arriving in this country over the years.

But if you do find a mention of your ancestors, particularly in the post-1844 naturalization files, you could be in for yet another of those genealogical treats. The Home Office made very thorough enquiries into the background of everyone applying to become a British citizen and the results of their investigations have been preserved in these files. Details such as age, place of birth, parentage and a physical description are usually given, together with information about how long the person has been in the UK and the various addresses they've lived at since their arrival. You should also expect to find testimonials from people who knew your ancestors and were willing to declare that they were suitable candidates for British citizenship. And the good news is that these files are now fully indexed and accessible via the National Archives' online catalogue, making searching for your immigrant ancestors easier than ever. The bad news, however, is that the vast majority of people arriving in the UK did not undergo the naturalization process. Nevertheless, since a search is now so easy to do there's really no excuse for not doing some exploring.

If you're fortunate enough to have Huguenot ancestry, you'll find that an enormous amount of material has been published by the Huguenot Society of Great Britain and Ireland. As well as the registers of the various Huguenot communities in England and Ireland, the Society has published volumes of indexes to *Letters of Denization and Acts of Naturalization, Lists of Aliens Resident in London* and *Returns of Strangers in the Metropolis,* all of which also include references to non-Huguenots.

This whole subject of naturalization and immigration is highly complex and there simply isn't the space to go into any real detail in a book of this size. For a more in-depth coverage see Roger Kershaw and Mark Pearsall's excellent guide, *Immigrants and Aliens: A Guide to Sources on UK Immigration and Citizenship,* which is published by the National Archives.

Share It

Since the 1970s, when public interest in family history began to grow, many thousands of people have researched their ancestors. Sadly, the result of much of this research is now lying in boxes in attics. All those notebooks and roughly drawn family trees, the certificates and census returns, copies of wills and clippings from newspapers – all lovingly and painstakingly researched and now gathering dust.

But it doesn't have to be like this: nowadays, publishing your family history is easier than you might think. You don't need to have access to expensive or hi-tech equipment and you don't have to negotiate a deal with a publisher. All you need is access to a computer, a touch of imagination and a bit of time on your hands.

The first thing to do is to get hold of a good family tree software package (there are several on the market, each of which works in much the same way and does much the same thing). You can use it to create family trees and to organise your data in a way that makes it easy to access – apart from anything else, this will help you to make the most of your trips to record offices and libraries. But perhaps the most useful aspect of your software package is that it will allow you to save your data in what is known as the GEDCOM (GEnealogical Data COMmunication) format. This was developed by the (Mormon) Church of Jesus Christ of Latter-day Saints in the 1980s and has become the 'industry standard' for handling family history data files.

Once you have a GEDCOM file of your family tree, sharing your research with others becomes a relatively straightforward matter and there are a number of different ways you can do it. The easiest is to send a copy of your GEDCOM file, either as an email attachment or saved onto a CD. However be warned that GEDCOM files can become quite big once you've keyed in your entire life's work (particularly if you've added a large number of photos), so unless both you and your recipient have a broadband internet connection you might want to consider another means of sharing your data. And remember that you should never attach a file of any sort when you're posting a message to a mailing list.

Another approach is to use one of the many websites that allow you to upload your GEDCOM file for the whole world to see. Before you do this you need to find out how your data will be displayed and what control you will have over it (can you make changes or even remove names?) and you might want to check that your files won't be used to someone else's commercial advantage. Another important point to bear in mind is that, as a rule, you shouldn' t publish information about living people.

The more adventurous among you might even consider creating your own websites; and don't ignore the power of the printed word - there are several companies that offer affordable solutions to publishing your research. Small print-runs of illustrated booklets can be a cheap and effective way of sharing your family's story with friends, relatives and other researchers.

The other side of the coin to all of this is that you can access the results of other people's research in any of the formats mentioned above. You may find that there are distant cousins out there who are researching the same people, and — you never know — they might have found their away around the brick wall that's been holding you up for months.

Finally, if there's no one in your family to carry on your research you might consider making a specific bequest in your will about what to do with your research once you've gone. The Society of Genealogists actively encourages people to arrange for their research (organised or not!) to be deposited in their library in London. So, act now and don't let your family history end up in a box, hidden away — or worse still, on a bonfire!

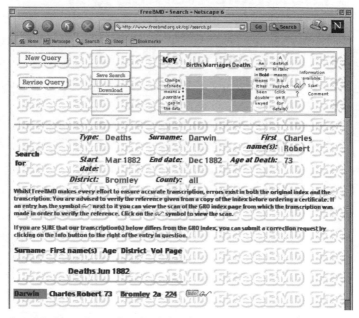

One of the increasing number of websites that are accelerating the pace of family history research.

Chapter 12

The whole world is out there: the World Wide Web

- Researching in cyberspace
- Good web technique
- Search engines
- Portals
- The individual and the web
- Mailing lists and message boards
- This ever changing world

Throughout this book you will have come across countless references to what has rapidly, over the past few years, become one of the most important resources for family historians – the World Wide Web.

Researching in cyberspace

It has been said that family history is the second most popular pursuit on the internet – no prizes for guessing what the *most* popular is – and it is hardly surprising that family history holds this position.

It's almost as if the World Wide Web was designed with family historians in mind. The way it enables people to share information, to ask questions and get quick answers, to interrogate vast databases and pull out the important information, to view the actual images of census pages and other documents written hundreds of years ago – all of this (and much more) makes the internet a truly indispensable tool.

And the amount of information out there is growing every day. Hardly a week passes without the launch of a new website offering access to yet another important source. Births, marriages and deaths, census returns, wills – websites offering indexes to these records and transcripts are now commonplace. But perhaps the biggest advance in recent years has been the development of sites which provide access to scanned digital images of original historical documents.

Family history websites can be divided into five basic types:

- sites giving access to digital images of primary source material, via an index;
- sites consisting of indexes to primary sources, sometimes with full transcripts;
- sites providing advice and guidance on using records;
- sites giving access to the results of an individual's personal research;
- sites providing links to other sites.

Viewing a scanned image of an original document is in many ways as good as looking at the real thing. You can view the document at your leisure and take your time to think about what it's telling you – and you're not relying on someone else's interpretation.

But some sites restrict you from browsing backwards and forwards through successive pages of the document – the digital equivalent of flicking through the pages – and this can make it difficult to understand how your page fits into the original context. A good researcher would always want to have a look at the census pages before and after the one that includes their ancestors, just to get a feeling for the type of area where they were living.

Although some of the websites that provide access to transcripts of original documents are undoubtedly a major asset to family history research, the details they give you are no substitute for viewing the document itself. And if the person who transcribed and indexed the document couldn't read a particular name, or if they made an error in the transcription, you might have real problems finding what you were looking for in the first place. Always check the original sources; think about where the information has come from; and most important of all, question everything.

Good web technique

Searching for our ancestors online has created a new rule for family historians:

Less is more

This is the mantra that you should repeat to yourself whenever you're searching for your ancestors in one of the big databases. Most of the search screens that you'll come across on family history websites are essentially the same: you get a variety of boxes inviting you to enter the name, age, place of birth and other details of the person that you're looking for. Some of the boxes have drop-down lists to make it even easier for you to complete them. And admit it: you're tempted to fill in every box, aren't you? After all, you know where your ancestor was born, so why shouldn't you enter it in that alluring little box at the bottom of the screen? You know that he would have been 35 at the time, so you put his age in too.

But by entering this additional information you're running the very real risk of eliminating the entry that you're actually looking for. Because, as we've seen, family history is not an exact science; our ancestors were not consistent about how they described their place of birth; the ages they gave were unreliable and often inaccurate, and most computer search engines are quite literal. If the information in the original document (never mind the transcript) is not entered exactly as you've just entered it into the search screen, you may struggle to find your person.

Let's take as an example a search in the 1901 Census Online website for someone who was born in Aldenham, Hertfordshire. You enter his name together with his place of birth, hit the search button and wait for a few seconds. What's your conclusion when the search fails to produce any results? That he's not in the records? That he was somehow missed by the enumerator? Possibly, but a good family historian never gives up, so you try again. This time you just put 'Aldenham' as the place of birth, but you still get no results. You try once more with no place of birth entered at all and now you get about twenty results – and there's your man, about halfway down the list. His place of birth is actually given as 'Radlett' (which was then a small hamlet situated in the parish of Aldenham), but because you've got a relatively short list of names to deal with you're able to identify him fairly easily.

So 'less is more' is your key to searching online databases. And unless you're looking for someone with quite a common name, you probably won't need to enter anything other than the person's name and possibly their age – allowing a year or two either side if the search screen allows you to do so. Your aim should be to produce a manageable list of names, and this may only be achieved after a certain amount of trial and error.

If you start out with too many results, try to think of ways of narrowing down your search; if you get none at all, or if your target is not on the list, remove some of the data that you've entered and try again. Most databases allow you to use what are known as 'wildcards' in your searches. This is where you use a symbol, usually the asterisk (*), question mark (?) or underscore (_), to stand for one or more characters in a word or even for nothing at all. So a search for SM?TH would produce entries for SMITH or SMYTH, while BROWN* would throw up BROWN as well as BROWNE and BROWNING. The use of wild-cards is sometimes restricted – you may have to enter at least two or three characters before you use one – but they can be a very powerful research tool if used wisely.

Always read the search tips on the website – each one works in a slightly different way, and if you want to get the best out of the search engine you need to make sure that you fully understand how it works.

So how do you find all this information that's out there? There are a number of different answers to that question, each of which has its advantages. The main two are:

- search engines such as Google
- 'portal' or 'directory' sites such as GENUKI or Cyndi's List

Search engines

These are the internet's gift to family historians. They allow us to find information about our ancestors in a way that was simply unimaginable just a few years ago. The effortless act of entering your name into a search engine can provide you with links to hundreds of websites containing references to that name – and all just a click away. Of course, the success of this basic approach depends very much on how common your name is – you wouldn't expect to get any meaningful results with names such as WILLIAMS or JONES. And if the surname is also a place name, a descriptive name or an occupation, like HAMPSHIRE, BROWN or BAKER, then you're going to have to think about adding some extra search terms: a first name, a place or even the words 'family history'.

This technique can produce effective results but you certainly shouldn't rely on it or think of it as a foolproof method of searching the internet. You need to be aware of a concept that is known as 'the invisible web' and you need to understand a little bit about how search engines gather their information. A search engine like Google uses a special type of robot programme called a spider to 'crawl' through the World Wide Web,

following links and retrieving as much information as it can from the pages it visits. When you
enter your search terms, Google checks its vast
database of over 8 billion web pages and presents you with a list of 'hits'. What the spider can't
do is type or think for itself, so when it encoun-
ters a search screen it is unable to interrogate it
in the way that you or I would.

When we carry out a search in an online database, the results we see are created on what is
known as a dynamic page – the page didn't exist
before we ran the search and it won't exist once
we close it down. The data itself is effectively
'invisible' to search engines. The online version
of the International Genealogical Index is a good
example. You may be able to find your great great
grandfather's baptism on the IGI but if you put his
name into Google you wouldn't find the relevant
entry in the list of results.

So you can't use search engines to search the
contents of an online database but you can
search *for* the database. Try typing in the subject
that you're interested in, and combine it with the
word 'database' and see what you get.

Portals

An alternative approach to finding information on the Internet is to use a portal site. The two most important for family historians are GENUKI at *www.genuki.org.uk* and Cyndi's List at *www. cyndislist.com*.

GENUKI (which stands for GENealogy UK and Ireland) is a vital resource for anyone with UK ancestry. The site is organized geographically. Each county has its own section with pages covering topics such as archives and libraries, church records, civil registration and maps. Although GENUKI does have much useful material of its own to offer the family historian, the main purpose of the site is to serve as a portal to other sites. The site is entirely run by volunteers and its coverage is understandably better for some counties than for others, but wherever your family came from, you're almost certain to find links to sites that you didn't even know existed.

Cyndi's List is an American site which works like a directory, each entry taking the form of a link to another website. Every conceivable family history topic has its own section and the range of subjects covered is quite simply astonishing. The site currently has nearly a quarter of a million links, and although much of this is dedicated to

American research, there's still some excellent coverage of UK sources.

Another useful portal site can be found at *www.familyrecords.gov*. This is a government site providing links to the websites of all of the national archive organizations in the United Kingdom as well as a number of other websites with significant national collections (such as the Commonwealth War Graves Commission) and some good basic information about researching your UK family history.

The individual and the web

The internet is also home to thousands of personal websites, and this aspect of the internet is both one of its strengths and one of its weaknesses. Most of these sites are made up of information that has been well researched and in some cases well documented – if you're lucky you may come across one that relates to your own ancestors, and this could open up new avenues of research for you and possibly even put you in contact with some distant cousins in California. But unfortunately there are also thousands of sites on the World Wide Web which contain research which is at best guesswork and at worst pure fabrication. There's a danger that

Did you know?
Nowadays, a growing number of researchers are extending their investigations beyond their own ancestors to research everyone with a particular surname. This approach to family history research (known as a One-Name Study) can help you to understand where your surname originated and how it developed and spread around the country.

once this sort of inaccurate information about an individual or a family is published on a website it assumes an authority and authenticity which is undeserved and is liable to be regurgitated on countless other sites. So, as with any other resources that you use in the course of your research, you should always check the source of the information, and if there doesn't seem to be one, treat it with extreme caution!

Mailing lists and message boards

Thanks to the internet it is now easier than ever to get in touch with other people who are researching the same surnames or even the same family as you. Message boards and mailing lists enable us to contact fellow researchers from all corners of the world and to share information with them – all in a matter of minutes and at the click of a mouse. It really couldn't be any easier.

There's a subtle difference between mailing lists and message boards. A mailing list is an interactive forum which you can subscribe to (for free) and then immediately post queries and receive (via email) messages that have been posted by other 'listers'. Then you simply sit back and wait for the answers to your query to drop into your inbox, and if you feel that you have something to contribute yourself, you can post your own replies to other messages. Don't forget about the time differences around the world and don't expect instant replies. If you're going to get any responses they'll probably appear within the first few days, but some people only check their emails at weekends so don't give up too soon.

Some lists are *very* busy. This is, of course, largely a good thing, but you may find that receiving twenty or thirty emails a day is just too much for you to cope with. Other lists have very little traffic and you may find that several days or even weeks pass without a message being posted. Most of the people who contribute to family history mailing lists are keen and enthusiastic researchers like you, but they may have been on the list for years and they may have developed an encyclopedic knowledge of the most important local sources. And you never know who you'll find on a mailing list – some of the world's leading experts on family history are regular contributors to mailing lists.

There are a few basic rules and guidelines that you should be aware of before you post your first message on a mailing list.

- Don't use html (hyper text markup language) or any fancy colours and fonts – plain text is always best.
- Never attach files to your messages – these can be harmful to other listers' PCs.
- Respect other people's views – you're quite free to disagree but keep it civilized.
- Don't expect people to do research for you without offering something in exchange.
- Don't post off-topic messages – make sure that your messages are relevant to the list.
- Don't post messages advertising a commercial product – it may be OK to mention a new publication as long as it's relevant, but be careful how you go about it!

Most mailing lists are monitored, and if inappropriate behaviour is detected the list owner will give the perpetrator a first warning. If they break the rules again they could find that their future posts are blocked.

All of this comes under the term 'netiquette',

which essentially means that you should observe the same standards of behaviour in cyberspace as you would practise in 'real life'.

Message boards work in a similar way to mailing lists but they allow you to post a message on a website which anyone can then see – people don't have to subscribe to a list in order to be able to read and respond to it. You're less likely to get quick answers to your queries, but searching message boards is pretty straightforward and you're quite likely to find some useful contacts out there.

Once you start looking around, you'll find that the range of subjects covered by family history mailing lists and message boards is huge. There are lists that cover whole counties or individual towns; there are lists dedicated to thousands of individual surnames; there are boards devoted to such topics as adoptions, DNA research, shipwrecks and medieval history. If a topic has a family history slant to it, you'll probably find a mailing list or a message board dedicated to it.

And by far the best way to find out about the vast range of these lists and message boards is to visit the biggest and best selection on the internet at *www.rootsweb.com*. Rootsweb currently boasts nearly 30,000 genealogy mailing lists and an immeasurable number of message boards. And if there isn't a board for your own surname you might want to consider starting one and becoming a board administrator. Rootsweb is also an excellent resource in its own right, with links to personal research pages and thousands of family trees that you can view online.

This ever changing world

The pace of change in the World Wide Web and information technology is now so fast, even in the 'sleepy' world of family history, that any attempt to document it must remain – in a para-doxical phrase – permanently provisional. But there are some good published guides to help you keep track of electronic developments, notably *The Genealogist's Internet* (3rd edition, 2005) by Peter Christian, published by the National Archives.

FamilyRecords.gov.uk
Your official source for family records

Home   Topics   Partners   Guides   Links   Help   Contact Info

Search: type here   GO

Welcome

This site, provided by the **FamilyRecords.gov.uk consortium**, aims to help you find the government records and other sources you need for your family history research.

The site is divided into two main sections: **Topics** and **Partners**. In the topics section you will find information on Births, Marriages & Deaths, Census, Migration etc. In the partners section, you will find information on each member of the FamilyRecords.gov.uk consortium.

Lost? use the **site map** to help you.

You can use **access keys** to navigate around this site - use **access key 0** for the list.

Focus on...

...Women in Uniform. Women have worked in diverse roles during wartime including nursing, teaching and farming and as clerks, fitters, cooks, pilots, drivers, anti-aircraft gun operators, decoders, RADAR operators and spies. We profile individual women and some of the organisations in which they served. **View the feature**   GO

NEWS AND EVENTS
Free family history talks

If you are new to family history and are able to get to central London, why not go to one of the free talks at the Family Record Centre? Tickets are issued on the day on a first-come, first-served basis more....

FIND OUT HOW TO GET A ...Census return

New to family history? We've written a guide for you - **start here.**

Looking for information on the Family Records Centre? **Go to FRC pages**

The Welcome screen of the UK government's FamilyRecords portal, which includes the National Archives and other bodies

In the end

We've come to the end of this book, but in some ways the journey has only just begun.

It's true that some people take up family history only to drop it after a few months, but most of us are in it for the long haul. Once you catch the bug it's difficult to shake off — and I'm not sure that anyone has ever found a cure.

You sometimes hear people saying that they finished researching their family tree years ago, which seems an odd statement to me. After all, since family history is essentially a process of working backwards through the generations, unless someone has successfully traced their ancestry back either to Adam and Eve or to the first micro-organism to emerge from the primordial soup (depending on your belief system) I don't really see how they *can* have finished.

And 'real' family historians never admit defeat. It's inevitable that from time to time in the course of your research you will come up against problems that you just can't solve, questions that you can't answer. But what you really mean is that you haven't found the answer to the problem *yet*. In the past year alone I have been fortunate enough to solve two problems in my own research which had been outstanding for almost twenty years — significantly, both as the result of information found on the internet. So don't give up: the answer *is* out there!

Researching your family history is supposed to be fun – I hope this book has convinced you of that, if nothing else. But I also hope that the need to take your research seriously has been brought home: the need to adhere to the principles of good research; to question the 'facts' that you unearth; to think logically about what you've discovered; and to understand how the vast range of historical documents that we've looked at can be used most effectively.

There's a danger that our family history research can become too important to us and that what begins as a harmless hobby can cross the line to become an obsession. We just need to make sure that it doesn't become an addiction. I haven't come across any branches of Family Historians Anonymous springing up around the country, but it may just be a matter of time! Seriously, you shouldn't let it take over your life – try not to turn your partner into a family history widow or widower.

But if you feel that you really need something to bridge the gap between the last visit to the Family Records Centre and the next, there are plenty of things you can do. Hundreds of books have been written on various aspects of family history research and there are now half a dozen or so magazines on the market. You can join your local family history society, which will almost certainly hold regular meetings, offering advice clinics and lectures as well as the opportunity to meet fellow researchers and share experiences.

Take time to explore the internet — you will be amazed by the amount of potentially useful material that's out there, just waiting to be discovered. Many people fear that the internet is making family history research too easy, and it's certainly true that you can do a lot of the basic research much more quickly than ever before. But surely this is a good thing if it gives us more time to investigate the more interesting records, those less obvious sources which make our hobby so worthwhile.

And many people also believe that the growth of the internet and the proliferation of online family history databases will be the death of archives. But there's certainly no sign of that happening so far, as visitor numbers at record offices around the country continue to grow. And I think that there are a number of very good reasons for this. For a start, the documents that can be accessed online represent a mere drop in the ocean compared to the volume of material in record offices that hasn't even been microfilmed, let alone digitally scanned. Second, record offices are home to some of the greatest minds in the archival world — where would family historians be without the help, advice and guidance of this great army of experts?

Finally, and I think most importantly of all, family history should be a social pursuit. No trip to a record office is complete without a lunch hour spent discussing your latest finds with a total stranger — although, of course, no serious family historian would ever stop for a whole hour!

So make the best of both worlds; embrace the internet and all it offers but don't forget the more traditional resources of the record offices. And whatever else you do, don't forget to enjoy your research and the pleasure of meeting like-minded people.

Glossary

Admon *See* LETTERS OF ADMINISTRATION.

Adoption The process of taking legal responsibility for another person's child.

Annuitant A person who receives a fixed sum of money at regular intervals.

Apportionments Documents produced to accompany TITHE MAPS, dating from around 1840 and listing owners and occupiers of land in each tithe district.

Apprentice A person who is learning a particular trade by working for someone else. *See also* JOURNEYMAN; MASTER.

Archdeaconry An administrative unit of the CHURCH OF ENGLAND.

Bachelor An unmarried man.

Banns The public declaration of the intent by two people to get married. The calling of banns in the parish church on three successive Sundays was introduced by the terms of HARDWICKE'S MARRIAGE ACT.

BIVRI British Isles Vital Records Index.

BL British Library.

Census An official count of the population. Carried out in the United Kingdom every ten years since 1801 (except 1941).

Census returns The records created as part of the process of taking a CENSUS.

Certificates Official documents recording major life events – i.e. births, marriages and deaths.

Church of England The established state church in England. Also referred to as the Anglican Church.

Church of Jesus Christ of Latter-day Saints The official name of the Mormon Church, founded in La Fayette, New York, in 1850 by Joseph Smith. Important to family historians for their network of FAMILY HISTORY CENTRES and the huge database known as the INTERNATIONAL GENEALOGICAL INDEX.

Civil registration The legal process of registering births, marriages and deaths introduced in England and Wales in 1837.

Clandestine marriage A term commonly used to describe marriages conducted by disreputable clergyman which took place in areas outside the control of the CHURCH OF ENGLAND. They were outlawed by the passing of HARDWICKE'S MARRIAGE ACT. Also known as IRREGULAR MARRIAGES.

Condition A category used in census returns, indicating whether married, single, widowed or divorced.

County record office A major repository holding important records relating to the people and history of a particular county.

CRO COUNTY RECORD OFFICE.

Deanery An administrative unit of the CHURCH OF ENGLAND.

Death duty A series of taxes raised by the INLAND REVENUE on the estate of the deceased.

Denization The act of making someone a citizen of the country. Originally the same as NATURALIZATION, but came to imply that citizenship had been granted by the Crown.

Diocese An administrative unit of the CHURCH OF ENGLAND.

Ecclesiastical Relating to the CHURCH OF ENGLAND.

Enumerator Official responsible for collecting and returning CENSUS information.

Family Bible A large Bible with pages for recording family events, notably births, marriages and deaths.

Family history centres A worldwide network of research centres provided by the CHURCH OF JESUS CHRIST OF LATTER-DAY SAINTS.

Family history society An organization formed to provide advice and guidance to family historians in a specific area. Most societies produce lists and indexes of relevant local material and hold regular meetings.

Family Records Centre An organization based in London, jointly run by the GENERAL REGISTER OFFICE and THE NATIONAL ARCHIVES. It provides access to some of the most important records for family historians in England and Wales including records of CIVIL REGISTRATION and CENSUS RETURNS.

FFHS Federation of Family History Societies. An umbrella organization representing the interests of local FAMILY HISTORY SOCIETIES.

First Avenue House The home of the Principal Registry of the Family Division, providing access to records of wills proved in England and Wales since 1858

FRC FAMILY RECORDS CENTRE.

Full age Aged 21 or over.

Genealogical Society of Utah The genealogical section of the CHURCH OF JESUS CHRIST OF LATTER-DAY SAINTS.

General Register Office Formed in 1837 to oversee the civil registration process. Also responsible for organizing census returns since 1861.

GENUKI A major website for family historians. Stands for **GEN**ealogy in the **U**nited **K**ingdom and **I**reland.

GRO GENERAL REGISTER OFFICE.

GRO indexes The indexes to births, marriages and deaths created by the GENERAL REGISTER OFFICE.

GSU GENEALOGICAL SOCIETY OF UTAH.

Hardwicke's Marriage Act An Act passed in 1753 which outlawed CLANDESTINE MARRIAGES in England and Wales.

HMC Historical Manuscripts Commission – now part of THE NATIONAL ARCHIVES.

Huguenots French Protestants who fled to England to escape religious persecution.

IGI INTERNATIONAL GENEALOGICAL INDEX.

Illegitimate A term used to describe a person whose parents are not legally married at the time of his or her birth.

Informant On a birth or death certificate, the person who provides the information to the REGISTRAR.

Inland Revenue A government board, formed in 1849, to collect various types of taxes.

International Genealogical Index A worldwide index compiled by the CHURCH OF JESUS CHRIST OF LATTER-DAY SAINTS. Contains millions of records of births, baptisms and marriages taken from a variety of sources.

Inventory A list of someone's personal possessions, made on their death, giving the value of each and the total value of the estate.

Irregular marriage *See* CLANDESTINE MARRIAGE.

Journeyman A person who is fully qualified to practise a particular craft or trade but is employed by another person. *See also* APPRENTICE; MASTER.

LDS Latter-day Saints. *See* the CHURCH OF JESUS CHRIST OF LATTER-DAY SAINTS.

Letters of administration A document granted by a court to those with a claim to the estate of someone who died without leaving a will. Commonly called an ADMON.

LMA London Metropolitan Archives.

Maiden surname A woman's surname before marriage.

Marriage licence A document issued by an ECCLESIASTICAL authority to a couple wishing to marry without the calling of BANNS.

Master A qualified craftsman, tradesman or artisan who employs others. *See also* APPRENTICE; JOURNEYMAN.

Mormon Church *See* the CHURCH OF JESUS CHRIST OF LATTER-DAY SAINTS.

The National Archives Formed in 2003 by the amalgamation of the PUBLIC RECORD OFFICE and the HISTORICAL MANUSCRIPTS COMMISSION.

Naturalization The act of making someone a citizen of the country. Originally the same as DENIZATION, but the term came to imply that citizenship was granted by Parliament.

Nonconformist Any Protestant who does not conform to the doctrines and usages of the established CHURCH OF ENGLAND.

OPR Old Parish Register, referring specifically to Scottish parish registers.

Parish registers Books kept by the Church of England to record the births (baptisms), marriages and deaths (burials) that took place within each parish. The main source for family historians prior to the introduction of CIVIL REGISTRATION in 1837.

PCC Prerogative Court of Canterbury.

PCY Prerogative Court of York.

Peculiar An administrative unit that is outside the normal ECCLESIASTICAL hierarchy.

PR PARISH REGISTER.

PRFD Principal Registry of the Family Division.

Primary sources Documents (such as CERTIFICATES and CENSUS RETURNS) which were created by recognized authorities such as the Church of England or the state.

PRO Public Record Office (now The National Archives).

Probate calendars Indexes to all wills proved in England and Wales, produced annually from 1858.

Province The senior administrative unit of the CHURCH OF ENGLAND. England is divided into two provinces: Canterbury and York. Until 1920, Wales was part of the province of Canterbury; but since then it has been an independent province, the Church in Wales.

Quakers *See* SOCIETY OF FRIENDS.

Quarters From 1837 until 1983, the GRO INDEXES for each year were divided into four quarters recording events registered between: January and March; April and June; July and September; and October and December. The quarters are commonly referred to by the last month.

Registrar A person appointed to register the births and deaths in a specified SUB-DISTRICT. Also responsible for performing civil marriage ceremonies.

Registration district An area established in 1837 as part of the CIVIL REGISTRATION process. England and Wales were divided into over 500 such districts. A Superintendent Registrar was appointed to be responsible for each district.

Relict The widow of a deceased man.

St Catherine's House An office in London, which, between 1973 and 1997, housed the GRO INDEXES.

Society of Friends A religious group founded by George Fox around 1650. Commonly known as QUAKERS.

Society of Genealogists A charity whose objects are to 'promote, encourage and foster the study, science and knowledge of genealogy'. Their library has a large collection of family histories, civil registration and census material, and a wealth of other material of use to family historians.

SoG SOCIETY OF GENEALOGISTS.

Spinster An unmarried woman.

Sub-district A sub-division of a REGISTRATION DISTRICT.

Three Denominations A group that was formed in 1789 to represent the political interests of the Baptist, Congregationalist and Presbyterian denominations.

Tithe maps Maps dating from around 1840, showing individually numbered parcels of land in each of the tithe district; linked with APPORTIONMENTS.

TNA THE NATIONAL ARCHIVES.

Trade directory A publication listing tradesmen and other residents, by address and occupation, usually within a specific town or county.

Widow A married woman whose husband is deceased.

Widower A married man whose wife is deceased.

Useful addresses

Borthwick Institute of Historical Research
University of York
York, YO10 5DD
Tel: 01904 642315
Website: www.york.ac.uk/inst/bihr

British Library Newspapers
Colindale Avenue
London, NW9 5HE
Tel: 020 7412 7353
Email: newspaper@bl.uk
Website: www.bl.uk/collections/
                newspapers.html

Church of Jesus Christ of Latter-day Saints
185 Penns Lane
Sutton Coldfield
West Midlands, B76 1JU
Tel: 0121 384 2028
Website: www.familysearch.org

Dr Williams's Library
14 Gordon Square
London, WC1H 0AR
Tel: 0207 387 3727
Email: enquiries@dwlib.co.uk
Website: www.dwlib.co.uk

Family Records Centre
1 Myddelton Street
London, EC1R 1UW
Tel: 0208 392 5300
Email: frc@nationalarchives.gov.uk
Website: www.familyrecords.gov.uk/frc

Federation of Family History Societies
Administrator
PO Box 2425
Coventry, CV5 6YX
Tel: 07041 492032
Email: info@ffhs.org.uk
Website: www.ffhs.org.uk

General Register Office
Certificate Services Section
PO Box 2
Southport, PR8 2JD
Tel: 0845 603 7788
Email: certificate.services@gro.gsi.gov.uk
Website: www.gro.gov.uk

General Register Office for Scotland
New Register House
Edinburgh, EH1 3YT
Tel: 0131 314 4433
Email: records@gro-scotland.gov.uk
Website: www.gro-scotland.gov.uk

Huguenot Society of Great Britain and Ireland
The Huguenot Library
University College
Gower Street
London, WC1E 6BT
Tel: 020 7679 5199
Email: secretary@huguenotsociety.org.uk
Website: www.huguenotsociety.org.uk

Hyde Park Family History Centre
64–68 Exhibition Road
South Kensington
London, SW7 2PA
Tel: 020 7589 8561

Institute of Heraldic and Genealogical Studies (IHGS)
79–82 Northgate
Canterbury
Kent, CT1 1BA
Tel: 01227 768664
Website: www.ihgs.ac.uk

London Metropolitan Archives
40 Northampton Road
London, EC1R 0HB
Tel: 020 7332 3820
Website: www.cityoflondon.gov.uk

The National Archives
Kew
Richmond
Surrey, TW9 4DU
Tel: 020 8876 3444
Website: www.nationalarchives.gov.uk

Principal Registry of the Family Division
Probate Search Room
First Avenue House
42–49 High Holborn
London, WC1V 6NP
Tel: 020 7947 7000
Email: cust.ser.cs@gtnet.gov.uk
Website: www.hmcourt-service.gov.uk
(Divorce Section   Tel: 020 7947 6000)

Society of Genealogists
14 Charterhouse Buildings
Goswell Road
London, EC1M 7BA
Tel: 020 7251 8799
Email: library@sog.org.uk
Website: www.sog.org.uk

Useful websites

www.1837online.com Access to the GRO's indexes to births, marriages and deaths in England and Wales as well as some census returns.

www.a2a.org.uk The Access to Archives database contains catalogues describing nearly 8 million items held in archives throughout England, dating from the 900s to the present day.

www.ancestry.co.uk An invaluable resource to genealogists researching the United Kingdom and Ireland .

www.archon.nationalarchives.gov.uk A list of UK repositories giving contact details and providing links to their websites.

www.cwgc.org Access the 'Debt of Honour Register', a database listing the 1.7 million men and women of the Commonwealth forces who died during the two world wars.

www.cyndislist.com A US-based, categorized and cross-referenced index to resources on the internet.

www.ellisisland.org Search the records of 22 million immigrants, passengers and crew members who passed through Ellis Island and the Port of New York between 1892 and 1924.

www.familyrecords.gov.uk A 'portal' site with links to official government sites for UK family history research, including the website of the Family Records Centre.

www.familysearch.org The Church of Latter-day Saints
website, including access to the International
Genealogical Index (IGI).

www.freebmd.org.uk Access to birth, marriage and
death indexes for England and Wales.

www.genuki.org.uk A comprehensive 'virtual reference
library' of information of particular relevance to the
UK and Ireland.

www.nationalarchives.gov.uk The website of The
National Archives, with access to the online catalogue and much more.

www.old-maps.co.uk Find out where your ancestors
lived and what their neighbourhood looked like over
a hundred years ago..

www.scotlandspeople.gov.uk An indispensable
resource for Scottish family history, providing access
to Scottish civil registration records, parish registers,
census returns and wills.

www.ukbmd.org.uk Links to websites offering online
indexes to records of UK births, marriages and
deaths

Further reading

G. Beech and R. Mitchell, *Maps for Family and Local Historians*, 2nd edn (The National Archives, 2004)

A. Bevan, *Tracing Your Ancestors in the National Archives*, 7th edn (National Archives, 2006)

G.R. Breed, *My Ancestors Were Baptists*, 4th edn (Society of Genealogists, 2002)

P. Christian, *The Genealogist's Internet*, 3rd edn (The National Archives, 2005)

D.J.H. Clifford, *My Ancestors Were Congregationalists*, 2nd edn (Society of Genealogists, 1997)

S. Colwell, *The Family Records Centre: A User's Guide* (The National Archives, 2002)

B. Dixon, *Birth and Death Certificates: England and Wales 1837 to 1969* (B. Dixon, 1999)

B. Dixon, *Marriage and Certificates in England and Wales* (B. Dixon, 2000)

M. Gandy, *Catholic Missions and Registers*, 6 vols (M. Gandy, 1993)

J. Gibson and E. Churchill, *Probate Jurisdictions: Where to Look for Wills*, 5th edn (Federation of Family History Societies, 2002)

J. Gibson and E. Hampson, *Marriage and Census Indexes for Family Historians*, 8th edn (Federation of Family History Societies, 2000)

J. Gibson and E. Hampson, *Specialist Indexes for Family Historians*, 2nd edn (Federation of Family History Societies, 2000)

J. Gibson and M. Medlycott, *Local Census Listings 1522–1930: Holdings in the British Isles*, 3rd edn (Federation of Family History Societies, 1997)

J. Gibson, B. Langston and B.W. Smith, *Local Newspapers 1750–1920: A Select Location List*, 2nd edn (Federation of Family History Societies, 2002)

K. Grannum and N. Taylor, *Wills and Other Probate Records* (The National Archives, 2004)

Guildhall Library, *The British Overseas: A Guide to Records of Their Births, Baptisms, Marriages, Deaths and Burials Available in the United Kingdom*, 3rd revised edn (Guildhall Library, 1994)

M. Herber, *Ancestral Trails* (Sutton, 1997)

D. Hey, *Journeys in Family History* (The National Archives, 2004)

E. Higgs, *Making Sense of the Census Revisited* (IHR/ The National Archives 2005)

C.R. Humphery-Smith, *The Phillimore Atlas & Index of Parish Registers*, 3rd edn (Phillimore, 2003)

R. Kershaw and M. Pearsall, *Immigrants and Aliens: A Guide to Sources on UK Immigration and Citizenship*, 2nd edn (The National Archives, 2004)

W. Leary, *My Ancestors Were Methodists* (Society of Genealogists, 1990)

E. Milligan and M. Thomas, *My Ancestors Were Quakers* (Society of Genealogists, 1999)

I. Mordy, *My Ancestors Were Jewish* (Society of Genealogists, 1995)

M. Nissel, *People Count: A History of the General Register Office* (HMSO, 1987)

A. Ruston, *My Ancestors Were English Presbyterians/ Unitarians* (Society of Genealogists, 1993)

Index